SEXAHOLICS ANONYMOUS®

SEXAHOLICS ANONYMOUS®

Library of Congress Cataloging-in-Publication Data

Sexaholics Anonymous.

1. Sexual addiction--Treatment. 2. Sexaholics Anonymous.
RC560.S43S48 1989 616.85'8306 89-10261
ISBN 978-0-9622887-3-9

Grateful acknowledgement is made for permission to reprint the following:

Excerpts from *Alcoholics Anonymous*. Copyright 1976 by Alcoholics Anonymous World Services, Inc. Reprinted by permission of Alcoholics Anonymous World Services, Inc.

Excerpts from *Twelve Steps and Twelve Traditions*. Copyright 1953 by Alcoholics Anonymous World Services, Inc. Reprinted by permission of Alcoholics Anonymous World Services, Inc.

First preliminary edition published 20 May 1984
Revised 1 July 1984
Revised 6 November 1984
Revised 5 May 1986
New and revised edition July 1989
Reprinted with footnote added to p. 192, 15 October 2001

The Problem

Many of us felt inadequate, unworthy, alone, and afraid. Our insides never matched what we saw on the outsides of others.

Early on, we came to feel disconnected—from parents, from peers, from ourselves. We tuned out with fantasy and masturbation. We plugged in by drinking in the pictures, the images, and pursuing the objects of our fantasies. We lusted and wanted to be lusted after.

We became true addicts: sex with self, promiscuity, adultery, dependency relationships, and more fantasy. We got it through the eyes; we bought it, we sold it, we traded it, we gave it away. We were addicted to the intrigue, the tease, the forbidden. The only way we knew to be free of it was to do it. "Please connect with me and make me whole!" we cried with outstretched arms. Lusting after the Big Fix, we gave away our power to others.

This produced guilt, self-hatred, remorse, emptiness, and pain, and we were driven ever inward, away from reality, away from love, lost inside ourselves.

Our habit made true intimacy impossible. We could never know real union with another because we were addicted to the *un*real. We went for the "chemistry," the connection that had the magic, *because* it by-passed intimacy and true union. Fantasy corrupted the real; lust killed love.

First addicts, then love cripples, we took from others to fill up what was lacking in ourselves. Conning ourselves time and again that the next one would save us, we were really losing our lives.

Contents

Preface

This book is for those who want to stop their sexually self-destructive thinking and behavior. It was written piece by piece as the need arose during the emergence and growth of Sexaholics Anonymous. The various pieces were loosely bound together by some early Sexaholics Anonymous groups and were later edited and printed in preliminary form in 1984. Demand for what came to be known as "the white book" has grown, and it is now being made available in this new and revised edition.

Sexaholics Anonymous is based on the principles of Alcoholics Anonymous. In this book we describe how these principles are working for us. When based on a foundation of sexual sobriety and put into personal action, the Twelve Steps and Traditions become the beginning of a whole new way of life. The longer we remain sober and grow in a fellowship of recovery, the more we learn about both the problem and the solution. We are still learning.

Sexaholics Anonymous came into being in the years 1979-1981. It is now a growing, international fellowship. The Twelve Step program, brought into the world through those finding victory over the tyranny of alcoholism, has become ours by the grace of God. We offer this book in the hope and prayer that it will continue to be blessed in the recovery of many from sexaholism.

To the Newcomer

What Works for Us

Those of us who are recovering in Sexaholics Anonymous were driven here by many different forms of the same problem. Some of us fit society's stereotypes of what a sexaholic might be and some of us did not. Some of us were driven to buy or sell sex on the streets, others to have it anonymously in bars or public places. Some of us found ourselves in painful and destructive affairs or consumed by an unhealthy obsession with a particular person or succession of persons. Many of us kept our obsessions to ourselves, resorting to compulsive masturbation, pictures, fetishes, voyeurism, or exhibitionism. Some of us victimized others. And with many of us, our compulsions took a toll on family, coworkers, and friends. Very often, we felt that we were the only ones who could not stop, that we were doing this—whatever it was—against our will.

When we came to SA, we found that in spite of our differences, we shared a common problem—the obsession of lust, usually combined with a compulsive demand for sex in some form. We identified with one another on the inside. Whatever the details of our problem, we were dying spiritually—dying of guilt, fear, and loneliness. As we came to see that we shared a common problem, we also came to see that for us, there is a common solution—the Twelve Steps of recovery practiced in a fellowship and on a foundation of what we call *sexual sobriety.* (See pp. 191-193.)

Our definition of sobriety represents, *for us*, the basic and necessary condition for lasting freedom from the pain that brought us to SA. We have found that nothing else works. When we have tried to deny what our common experience has taught us, we have found that recovery still eludes us. And this seems to be true whether we are male or female; married or single; whether our acting out was with the same or opposite sex; whether our relationships were "committed," "meaningful," or one-night stands; or whether we just resorted to a little sex with self as a "physical outlet." As the men and women of Alcoholics Anonymous learned over fifty years ago, "half-measures availed us nothing"!

We don't claim to understand all the ramifications of sexual sobriety. Some of us have come to believe that there is a deeper spiritual significance in sexual sobriety, while others simply report that without a firm and clear bottom line, our "cunning, baffling, and powerful" sexaholism takes over sooner or later. Nor do we claim that sobriety *alone* will lead to a lasting and joyous recovery. Like alcoholics, we can be "dry" without being sober in a deeper sense. We don't even claim that sexual sobriety will make one feel better immediately. We, like other addicts, can go through withdrawal symptoms when we give up our "drug." Nonetheless, in spite of the questions, struggles, and confusion that we have gone through, we find that sexual sobriety is truly "the key to a happy and joyous freedom we could otherwise never know." That's why we keep coming back to SA.

We have a solution. We don't claim that it's for everybody, but for us, it works. If you identify with us and think you may share our problem, we'd like to share our solution with you.

A Caution

We suggest that newcomers to Sexaholics Anonymous *not* reveal their sexual past to a spouse or family member who does not already know of it, without careful consideration and a period of sexual sobriety, and even then, only after prior discussion with an SA sponsor or group. Typically, when we come into the program, we want to share our excitement with those closest to us and tell all right away. Such disclosures might injure our family or others and should be confined to the group of which we are a part until a wise course is indicated. Of course, if there is any chance we have put others in danger, we take immediate steps to try to correct that.

Few things can so damage the possibility of healing in the family as a *premature* confession to spouse or family where sacred bonds and trust have been violated. Unwittingly, such confessions can be attempts on our part to dump our guilt, get back into good graces, or make just another show of willpower. Great caution is advised here.

Amends to family must begin with a sexually sober, changed attitude and behavior on a daily basis. Then, as we grow in recovery, we will find how to make direct amends. Help from sponsor and group is indispensable here. There's always a way, if we really want to make things right.

What Is a Sexaholic and What Is Sexual Sobriety?

We can only speak for ourselves. The specialized nature of Sexaholics Anonymous can best be understood in terms of what we call the *sexaholic*. The sexaholic has taken himself or herself out of the whole context of what is right or wrong. He or she has lost control, no longer has the power of choice, and is not free to stop. Lust has become an addiction. Our situation is like that of the alcoholic who can no longer tolerate alcohol and must stop drinking altogether but is hooked and cannot stop. So it is with the sexaholic, or sex drunk, who can no longer tolerate lust but cannot stop.

Thus, *for the sexaholic*, any form of sex with one's self or with partners other than the spouse is progressively addictive and destructive. We also see that lust is the driving force behind our sexual acting out, and true sobriety includes progressive victory over lust. These conclusions were forced upon us in the crucible of our experiences and recovery; we have no other options. But we have found that acceptance of these facts is the key to a happy and joyous freedom we could otherwise never know.

This will and should discourage many inquirers who admit to sexual obsession or compulsion but who simply want to control and enjoy it, much as the alcoholic would like to control and enjoy drinking. Until we had been driven to the point of despair, until we really wanted to stop but could not, we did not give ourselves to this program of recovery. Sexaholics Anonymous is for those who know they have no other option but to stop, and their own enlightened self-interest must tell them this.

What Is Sexaholics Anonymous?

Sexaholics Anonymous is a fellowship of men and women who share their experience, strength, and hope with each other that they may solve their common problem and help others to recover. The only requirement for membership is a desire to stop lusting and become sexually sober. There are no dues or fees for SA membership; we are self-supporting through our own contributions. Sexaholics Anonymous is not allied with any sect, denomination, politics, organization, or institution; does not wish to engage in any controversy; neither endorses nor opposes any causes. Our primary purpose is to stay sexually sober and help other sexaholics to achieve sobriety.

The Twelve Steps of Alcoholics Anonymous

1. We admitted we were powerless over alcohol—that our lives had become unmanageable. 2. Came to believe that a Power greater than ourselves could restore us to sanity. 3. Made a decision to turn our will and our lives over to the care of God *as we understood Him.* 4. Made a searching and fearless moral inventory of ourselves. 5. Admitted to God, to ourselves, and to another human being the exact nature of our wrongs. 6. Were entirely ready to have God remove all these defects of character. 7. Humbly asked Him to remove our shortcomings. 8. Made a list of all persons we had harmed, and became willing to make amends to them all. 9. Made direct amends to such people wherever possible, except when to do so would injure them or others. 10. Continued to take personal inventory and when we were wrong promptly admitted it. 11. Sought through prayer and meditation to improve our conscious contact with God *as we understood Him,* praying only for knowledge of His will for us and the power to carry that out. 12. Having had a spiritual awakening as the result of these Steps, we tried to carry this message to alcoholics, and to practice these principles in all our affairs.

The Twelve Traditions of Alcoholics Anonymous

1. Our common welfare should come first; personal recovery depends upon AA unity. 2. For our group purpose there is but one ultimate authority—a loving God as He may express Himself in our group conscience. Our leaders are but trusted servants; they do not govern. 3. The only requirement for AA membership is a desire to stop drinking. 4. Each group should be autonomous except in matters affecting other groups or AA as a whole. 5. Each group has but one primary purpose—to carry its message to the alcoholic who still suffers. 6. An AA group ought never endorse, finance, or lend the AA name to any related faclity or outside enterprise, lest problems of money, property, and prestige divert us from our primary purpose. 7. Every AA group ought to be fully self-supporting, declining outside contributions. 8. Alcoholics Anonymous should remain forever nonprofesisonal, but our service centers may employ special workers. 9. AA, as such, ought never be organized; but we may create service boards or committees directly responsible to those they serve. 10. Alcoholics Anonymous has no opinion on outside issues; hence the AA name ought never be drawn into public controversy. 11. Our public relations policy is based on attraction rather than promotion; we need always maintain personal anonymity at the level of press, radio, and films. 12. Anonymity is the spiritual foundation of all our Traditions, ever reminding us to place principles before personalities.

The Twelve Steps of Sexaholics Anonymous

1. We admitted that we were powerless over lust—that our lives had become unmanageable.
2. Came to believe that a Power greater than ourselves could restore us to sanity.
3. Made a decision to turn our will and our lives over to the care of God as we understood Him.
4. Made a searching and fearless moral inventory of ourselves.
5. Admitted to God, to ourselves, and to another human being the exact nature of our wrongs.
6. Were entirely ready to have God remove all these defects of character.
7. Humbly asked Him to remove our shortcomings.
8. Made a list of all persons we had harmed, and became willing to make amends to them all.
9. Made direct amends to such people wherever possible, except when to do so would injure them or others.
10. Continued to take personal inventory and when we were wrong promptly admitted it.
11. Sought through prayer and meditation to improve our conscious contact with God as we understood Him, praying only for knowledge of His will for us and the power to carry that out.
12. Having had a spiritual awakening as the result of these Steps, we tried to carry this message to sexaholics and to practice these principles in all our affairs.

The Twelve Traditions of Sexaholics Anonymous

1. Our common welfare should come first; personal recovery depends on SA unity.
2. For our group purpose there is but one ultimate authority—a loving God as He may express Himself in our group conscience. Our leaders are but trusted servants; they do not govern.
3. The only requirement for membership is a desire to stop lusting and become sexually sober.
4. Each group should be autonomous except in matters affecting other groups or Sexaholics Anonymous as a whole.
5. Each group has but one primary purpose—to carry its message to the sexaholic who still suffers.
6. An SA group ought never endorse, finance, or lend the SA name to any related facility or outside enterprise, lest problems of money, property, and prestige divert us from our primary purpose.
7. Every SA group ought to be fully self-supporting, declining outside contributions.
8. Sexaholics Anonymous should remain forever nonprofessional, but our service centers may employ special workers.
9. SA, as such, ought never be organized; but we may create service boards or committees directly responsible to those they serve.
10. Sexaholics Anonymous has no opinion on outside issues; hence the SA name ought never be drawn into public controversy.
11. Our public relations policy is based on attraction rather than promotion; we need always maintain personal anonymity at the level of press, radio, films, and television.
12. Anonymity is the spiritual foundation of all our traditions, ever reminding us to place principles before personalities.

Twenty Questions

__ 1. Have you ever thought you needed help for your sexual thinking or behavior?
__ 2. That you'd be better off if you didn't keep "giving in"?
__ 3. That sex or stimuli are controlling you?
__ 4. Have you ever tried to stop or limit doing what you felt was wrong in your sexual behavior?
__ 5. Do you resort to sex to escape, relieve anxiety, or because you can't cope?
__ 6. Do you feel guilt, remorse, or depression afterward?
__ 7. Has your pursuit of sex become more compulsive?
__ 8. Does it interfere with relations with your spouse?
__ 9. Do you have to resort to images or memories during sex?
__10. Does an irresistible impulse arise when the other party makes the overtures or sex is offered?
__11. Do you keep going from one relationship or lover to another?
__12. Do you feel the right relationship would help you stop lusting, masturbating, or being so promiscuous?
__13. Do you have a destructive need—a desperate sexual or emotional need for someone?
__14. Does pursuit of sex make you careless for yourself or the welfare of your family or others?
__15. Has your effectiveness or concentration decreased as sex has become more compulsive?
__16. Do you lose time from work for it?
__17. Do you turn to a lower environment when pursuing sex?
__18. Do you want to get away from the sex partner as soon as possible after the act?
__19. Although your spouse is sexually compatible, do you still masturbate or have sex with others?
__20. Have you ever been arrested for a sex-related offense?

A Personal Story

What was it like? I hope I never forget, for if I do, I'm liable to go right back out there and think I can lust like a gentleman again. You see, I'm a sexaholic, a recovering sex drunk. That's like an alcoholic, only the drug is sexual lust instead of booze.

As a small child, I was a thumb sucker, and the only way my parents could rid me of the habit was to call in the local motorcycle cop. It was the 1930s, in the country not far from Los Angeles. My parents, who came to America on the high tide of immigration, ran a small neighborhood store, a combination gas station, shoe repair, and grocery. There in our store I was confronted with the ultimatum from this giant Enforcer, who loomed so large over me all I can remember is his huge potbelly and Sam Browne belt. It was either stop sucking my thumb or he would start slicing pieces off the end. I stopped, with a convulsive shudder. But I *needed* that pacifier.

The only other obsessions I can remember before age eight were the Sunday comics and evening radio adventure stories and mysteries. My brother and I would practically crawl inside the loudspeaker to lose ourselves in total fantasy and escape the harsh realities of Depression poverty, which took our father and left mother with three hungry excuses for anxious desperation.

My favorite comic strip was Flash Gordon, with its brave men, marvelous machines, and gorgeous women in stunning and revealing costumes. One Sunday I was devouring the strip with gaping soul when Azura the Queen of Magic appeared out of nowhere to embrace Flash and touch my childhood—a strange new experience. The sexual arousal gave me the means of flight from reality, and I found myself compelled to escape daily into the ecstatic oblivion that masturbation provided. I had found my "connection"; it was imprinted from the very beginning, and sex would thereafter become dependent on picture-women.

Though developing normally physically, I stopped maturing emotionally. In grammar school I wanted so to break through and relate to other children, but never quite made it. I just wasn't there. I was off somewhere hiding inside myself, peering out at the world like it was all just another show being imagined in my head. Loss of emotional control was also evident during this period, and in ensuing years, in fits of temper, I would vent my suppressed resentment and strike out in violence against my brother.

Junior high school was more of the same, only with more anxiety. Boys and girls were pairing off, but I felt like the misfit, still peering out at the world. And masturbation—always masturbation. I used it as a pacifier, soporific, for escape, and for feeling I was really alive. High school was the worst. I remember girls wanting me, but I still couldn't break through. I had a crush on a girl, but the best I could manage was looking at her when she couldn't see me looking. It was in high school where I began seeing what was really going on between the sexes, secretly yearning for some of the action, not yet knowing what "it" really was. So I stole the locked supplement to the biology textbook and discovered to my great surprise and pleasure how humans had sex with each other. That's learning the hard way for someone who'd been a sex drunk for nine years!

In high school some of us would work half a day in the aircraft industry, then go to school the rest of the day. I remember bucking rivets on bombers, where the back-alley talk did more to feed my lust than pictures ever did. Part of me wanted what was on the wild side and wouldn't be satisfied without it, religious upbringing notwithstanding. That, plus a few brief encounters with high school temptresses—I see now they may have been captive to lust too—lit the fuse of desire that would smolder for years to come. I was extremely allergic to lust all along but never knew it. I just had that devastating feeling of being different.

Whatever else was going on in those years, two things were as certain as my own existence, maybe more so—the daily need for my sexual "drug" to ease the emotional turmoil inside and the continuing search for pictures to feed the idolatrous craving.

A New Phase

The U.S. Navy was the first time I can remember trying seriously to stop masturbating. Sensing something must be wrong, I brought huge hunks of willpower into play, along with new religious convictions. But all that did was turn me into a "periodic." (That's the term alcoholics use to describe the kind of drinking some of them did. Daily drinkers keep a certain level in their system; periodics can go without alcohol for days, weeks, or months, then binge.) I would force myself to go a few days or so without resorting to masturbation. After all, I was a man now, wasn't I? But this new pattern only worsened the inner conflict and fed my denial that there was a real problem.

After the Navy I entered college and worked summers in the aircraft industry. What a tremendous surprise to discover the stand around the corner where I could buy a whole magazine full of women! I could have my Queen of Magic—and better—whenever I wanted. Like the alcoholic, I had to know a "drink" was available at all times. This was my lifeline. At this stage, I don't think I was lusting after women in the flesh yet; lust was still tied to images on paper or in my fantasy. But having a ready supply handy only intensified the problem. The more I knew was available, the more I wanted and had to have, resulting in the need to "change partners" more frequently. As this new practice progressed, I found myself using a magazine, then destroying it. Tearing it up and throwing it away meant I was swearing off, never to do it again. Again and again and again! What better way of supporting denial? How all this damaged my ability to *relate* to a woman—or to anyone—would only become apparent to me half a lifetime later.

As I fed my malady and it progressed, so did the pictures in the magazines. There was always that enticing revelation of more and better and wilder pulling me on. It was as though lust had to keep advancing, and, never satisfied, had to resort to the ever-more-explicit images on which to feed. I'm a walking history of the rise of the men's magazines. In a way, my lust helped bring them into being. And, of course, they aided and abetted my lust. Lust always wanted more.

Once a new threshold was crossed—my first was women in one-piece bathing suits!—there was a new drug I had to have. But it only worked long enough for the next one to come along and carry me a step further. And as soon as that line was crossed, the next appeared as if by magic and *had* to be crossed. That addictive wave kept on advancing. It never stopped. There was always a new enticing aspect of Desire out there—or is it in here?—ready and waiting to pull me into it. And I had to keep riding the leading edge of that wave. The more there was, the more I wanted. The more I wanted, the more I had to have. Wanting more always led to wanting more!

The first semester in college was good. My brother and I were reunited, college was exciting, masturbation was working, and I was doing well. Then a local minister intervened and manipulated what he thought would be a good boy-girl match. After all, we both played the violin, didn't we? I had never even gone out with a girl before, but shortly found myself engaged to be married! Twenty years old on the outside, I was an emotionally stunted child-adolescent on the inside. The poor girl must have thought she was trying to relate to a whirlwind. But the hurricane of events and my own confused emotions swept *me* off my feet; I don't even remember how it happened. I do remember swearing off sex with myself for a month during the engagement. It was the longest I'd ever gone without, and I did it by sheer fighting—white-knuckling it. But it fought back, naturally, and being deprived of the only "drug" I had at the time, I came close to a nervous breakdown. This engagement was interfering with my "drinking" something awful, so I found a perfect excuse to start up again. Big M—the good old unmentionable. How could I have thought I could ever live without it?

Marriage

Then marriage. What a shock! Somewhere in St. Paul, Minnesota, in a tiny upstairs bedroom large enough for only one bed, dents from pounding my head against the wall next to that bed from sexual frustration are probably still in the plaster. Finally, after a misunderstanding about not having babies, we had sex together. For the first time in my life I had sex with a woman. It was wonderful. So much better than masturbation! I wouldn't have to do that anymore! Free at last! And what a glorious feeling, being united with a woman. This was finally the answer I'd been looking for. I was in for another shock.

It turned out that I could not make the transition from auto-sex to union with another. Lust allowed me that honeymoon for a short time, only to demand its due again later. My old programming of twelve years was still there; I hadn't changed. Lust proved stronger than love (whatever that was). My jealous "true love," Lust, would not let me go so easily. Masturbation again. Then, very soon, I began looking at, then wanting other girls. One partner, just like one picture, would never satisfy. I began wanting in the flesh what I had been programming my lust for in all those picture-affairs. That's when the fuse caught fire and began burning toward the powder keg.

Expecting a child, we returned to California, where my wife could be closer to home. I wanted to finish college, so after the baby came, we lived in the veterans' housing project on university campus. It was then I started taking off my wedding band so girls wouldn't see I was married. Another stage in the progression had arrived. I began the pursuit. First on campus, then on the sidewalks of the city, then downtown skid row. I think I was trying to hide even from myself what I was really after, but I found it nevertheless. They called them B-girls—bait used to lure men into bars to consume watered-down drinks. That first time, I went through all the grocery money in a few minutes, hoping I'd be offered something else more potent.

That's when the fireworks began. Desire, which had hitherto been inside my head only, began breaking out. Being powerless over masturbation was nothing compared with this. It was a thousandfold more intense. Lust exploded within me like the star-burst from a Fourth of July rocket.

By age twenty-six I had scored my first adulterous affair. And lightning didn't strike me dead! What a wonderful freedom! I could enjoy adultery; I reveled in it. Free at last! What great release from that prison-house of the mind, where it had all been repressed fantasy and dammed-up desire. Liberated! I had finally broken free. Affairs followed, one after another. Ah, the romance. "Dancing in the Dark. . . ." But adultery, even without guilt, didn't solve my problem either. I didn't know that lust itself was my problem, and that everything I was thinking and doing in the sexual area was only making it worse.

Another Stage

Then one night, out of nowhere, a prostitute jumped into my car. Was I ready! *This* was what I'd really been waiting for. The Queen of Magic in the flesh! This new ecstasy would *surely* lead me out of bondage into reality. No more masturbation. No more complicated affairs or pseudo-romantic preludes. No strings. What a glorious freedom! Little did I know that again, I was hooked from the very first, never again free *not* to resort to prostitutes, just as from the first I was never free not to resort to masturbation or adultery. The malady had advanced yet another stage. Another invisible line had been crossed.

At this time I was in seminary studying theology and working as an assistant in a local church. Everything seemed to pile up on me all at once. For one thing, I couldn't stand living the lie anymore, preaching and teaching the "Answer," yet secretly living in total bondage. And the addiction had destroyed my marriage. Lust always came first. Living with others, much less being responsible, was impossible. My life had become unmanageable. So after twelve years of tumultuous marriage and three beautiful children, I ran. It was just as well. The chaos I'd let loose inside my own heart and soul was wreaking havoc in my wife and children. Lust, like alcoholism, I later came to see, is a family disease. Everyone tied to the sex drunk is affected. Thus, one day I simply walked out on everything—bolted is more like it—from seminary, ministry, marriage, and family. That I wound up almost bolting from life is another matter.

Now the pursuit shifted to the seamier side of town, and by thirty-five I was a dyed-in-the-wool compulsive "trick," the term hookers use for their customers. I was descending into the demimonde of prostitutes, pimps, panderers, and associated vice and criminality. At times, for security, I carried a concealed folding machete with an eleven-inch blade. God only knows how close I came to being pulled into that dark whirlpool and getting sucked under completely.

But I thought it was great, that this was "where it was really at." I never suspected that the whole process from the very beginning was creating a deadly false reality and short-circuiting my ability to have normal relationships with anyone, let alone wife and children. Without sensing what was happening anywhere along the line, the great love "maker" had become the great love cripple.

Out of Control

Even my pursuit of sex on the streets progressed downhill. At first, it would only be under certain conditions or with a certain type of prostitute, and always with protection against disease. But one by one, over time, every single constraint and taboo was crossed. The more I indulged, the broader the spectrum of possibilities for feeding the obsession, including crossing the gender line.

I must have felt the slavery. Once I was arrested by vice officers and hauled out onto the sidewalk for the whole world to gape at. I wished I could have disappeared! While they were frisking me, spread-eagled against the graffiti-blackened brick wall, I was saying to myself, Thank God! This is what I needed to make me stop. Never again! But it wasn't five minutes after my release that I was back out there looking for the same woman. Any woman!

Another time I was driving on the freeway. The compulsion had struck, I had quickly cashed a check and was racing out to the red-light district, when I saw a man lose control of his car and spin off into the center divider, slamming into it just as I whizzed by inches away. His car struck the divider from the rear, and I saw his head jerk over the back of his seat and snap completely back in a grotesque U-shape, obviously breaking his neck. I pulled off the next ramp, shaken, acknowledging the incident as a warning from heaven. Thank God! I thought, That's what I needed to make me stop. Never again! Less than a minute later, however, I found my car getting back onto the freeway, heading for its original scarlet assignation.

I had lost control of *me*. The compulsion had complete control, as it always had, from the very first. Only this was no longer "innocent." Lust was taking on a malevolent aspect. I was getting perilously close to connecting with the Darkness and crossing the point of no return. Those who've been out there know what I mean. After awhile, it ceases to be fun and games; it's for keeps.

But I thought I was free. Free from the yoke of marriage and responsibility. How easy to forget the family even existed. Free to pursue lust as I wished without having to creep home guiltily, fearing discovery. But the more freedom I had, the less free I became. The escape that the ritual and sex provided wasn't as complete and didn't last as long as before. The pleasure was not as unsullied, the rapture not as naive. I must have begun to see. I would swear off prostitutes periodically. Sex with myself had never stopped, and the magazines kept apace to feed the progression, abetting it further still. Then I'd try to stay completely sober without either. Nothing worked longer than a few weeks at best.

Somewhere, again, I had crossed another invisible line. Lust, by which I had been able to function and for which I lived, was exacting a wage—from *me*. Each new stage brought increased craving, which brought ever greater dependence and more insatiable desire and an ever greater need to quit.

About this time, I was beginning to look for a way out again; my ability to function and cope was deteriorating. Few realize what a terrible toll this thing takes on a person. But none of the professionals I went to for help caught on to the real problem. And I still had no idea what the real problem was. The problem was always "out there"—wife, children, other people, the boss, the job, institutions, religious hypocrisy. After the divorce I had gone to a psychoanalyst, only to be reassured that my new career with prostitutes was merely relieving a natural urge. Boy, did I want to hear that! Later I would try other psychiatrists and group therapies. I never heard there might be such a thing as compulsive sex, much less that it could be addictive, progressive, and destructive. Later, when I remarried, one psychiatrist insisted I simply wasn't getting enough at home. But my wife and I were compatible sexually, and I got as much as I went after, and more.

Free at Last?

What insights I did get into my motivations only seemed to add to the curse, much as did my religious knowledge and belief. Knowledge was not power—even right knowledge! What I needed was not more knowledge about my psychology or God, but power to stop what I was powerless over and obey the little light I already had. I had stopped thousands of times; almost every time was the "last time." *Staying* stopped was my problem, and I made countless vain attempts at that: churches, prayer, fasting, therapy, tranquilizing drugs, and then remarriage, a new home, and a new job. What I really needed, I thought, was the right woman, the right job, and the right environment in which to live and work.

In the new marriage I got all three. And on my wedding day I burned all my girlie magazines and movies in one grand show of willpower and high resolve. But it was like cutting off part of me, so dear were those favorite goddesses of mine. Within days after the wedding I was back to masturbation, and within months I was back on the streets, helplessly sinning against the new light of love, kindness, plenty, and peaceful surroundings. I must have sensed something was drastically wrong with me, but if I did, it didn't do any good. And the wives never guessed the darkest secret locked in their husband's heart. Lust was his one and only wife, mistress, goddess, and slave master, and he was chained for life. My wives had never stood a chance!

I had decided to quit my job of ten years, thinking that if only I could do what I really wanted—write—all would be well with me. So we sold our home, and I got away from it all. I realized later that one reason I had quit my job was to avoid having an affair with a woman at work. It was another gallant and courageous attempt to do it on my own. Quitting the job was scary, but I felt great; it would be a new beginning. Free at last from all those temptations at work and free from the rat race, I could hide away in my niche full of books and become something new and better and different.

Despair

But that didn't work either. Stealing away, I'd race into the big city, score a connection, and return undetected. I just couldn't believe it; I had given it my best shot. I was doing what I wanted to do in an ideal situation, surrounded by love and nurturing, and yet I kept on going downhill! (If these good wives only knew how they were nurturing and supporting the sickness!) I began to see that all those great feelings of release and freedom that had accompanied the progression of the malady had been delusions. I had no idea that I was deluding myself, creating my own insanity. One stage at a time, I had been seducing and victimizing myself into a great lie: The Wages of Lust Is Life. I had never come to terms with the true nature of my problem: The wages of lust is death.

I progressed in the lie until finally, even the thought of masturbation or merely looking at a girlie magazine cover in the liquor store or supermarket ignited the compulsion, and I would have to go out and score my "drug"—find a prostitute. As this pattern of periodic despair worsened relentlessly, I finally concluded I had to be possessed with demons and submitted to the rite of exorcism. I thought I was willing to go to any lengths to stop the insanity.

Well, exorcism didn't work either. I even contemplated a drastic variation on the motorcycle cop routine. (Yes, I was getting that desperate!) There was nothing left for me to try; there was nowhere else to go and still be in charge, managing my will and life. I see now that in all my religious striving and psychotherapy I was waiting for the miracle to happen *first*, that I should somehow be zapped or "fixed," unable ever to fall or be tempted again. I thought that if a person just had the right religious belief, he was automatically "a new creature; old things are passed away; behold, all things are become new." That all thought of lust would be removed, much as a tumor would be excised by a surgeon. The "religious solution" was one of the subtlest strategies in my arsenal of denial.

I didn't realize that the essence of being human is to have free choice. God doesn't want to remove from me the possibility of falling; he wants me to have the freedom to *choose* not to fall. I'd been praying self-righteously all along, "Please God, take it away!" not realizing my inner heart was piteously whining, ". . . so I won't have to give it up." There was *belief* in God without surrender. That belief availed nothing! I had never died to lust.

The Dawn of Freedom

It wasn't long after this, in 1974, that I went to the mailbox and found the April 22nd issue of *Time* magazine. Its cover story was on The New Alcoholism. I sat down, devoured the article, got up, and called Alcoholics Anonymous. Many things in the article had struck with the force of revelation: There were many "alcoholisms"; it was being called a disease; it was hitting men and women, old and young alike; the descriptions of powerlessness matched my own; treatment, described by some professionals, was like trying to "exorcise a host of demons." Medicine, psychotherapy, and psychoanalysis didn't work. Alcoholics Anonymous did.

I went to my first meeting that night. That's how I discovered that the AA program of recovery for alcoholics would work for a sex drunk. And I was just as hopeless a drunk as any wino on skid row. I'd been there. In my very first meeting I saw people as desperate over alcohol as I was over lust, living free of their obsession. Here was a program of recovery that was working for them. And it has been working for me ever since, whenever I work it or let it work me.

I admitted gladly what I must have known all along, that I was powerless over lust, just like alcoholics were powerless over alcohol. The paradox made immediate sense: To win, I had to surrender and admit defeat.

I put down lust as one would put down heroin or alcohol. For me that meant not feeding it through the eye or in the mind. I also abstained from all sex, including with my wife. The second marriage was on the verge of collapse anyway. I wasn't even afraid sexual withdrawal would kill me, as I had felt before. I simply knew I had to stop, no matter what the cost. A strange thing happened; I didn't die! Why hadn't anyone ever told me that sex was optional?

I began going to AA meetings, stopped drinking and taking tranquilizers, and read the book *Alcoholics Anonymous*. I identified with the alcoholics right down the line.

After a few months I began having sex with my wife again, and not long thereafter discovered an amazing thing—sex without lust. They were two entirely different things! Intercourse without stimulation or an arousal scenario playing in my mind was something I had never known before. It was very simple, natural, real, and satisfying. What a gift!

But I soon discovered something else: it was too rare a thing. The pattern was that even though I was having sex only with my wife and had withdrawn from feeding lust at other times, I was still resorting to memories of pictures or past encounters to achieve arousal and orgasm. I wasn't free of my past, even though I was apparently free of the sexual compulsion in its old "scarlet" forms. What was wrong? Wouldn't everything be all right as long as I didn't take that first "drink"? But what was drinking for the alcoholic wasn't drinking for me, the sexaholic. To be fully free, I'd have to be free even of resorting to other partners in my mind. And for me, this was a long time in coming. I would discover slowly that my mental habit patterns were the key to my illness; without healing here, there would be no real recovery.

But here again, I found I was just as powerless over the images in my memory as I had been in my compulsive pursuit of sex. The more I tried to force the memories away, the harder they fought to stay alive. I would have to begin working the Twelve Steps of recovery for the *inner* man. But I delayed, and delay was almost fatal. After a year and a half without acting out the old sexual compulsion, I fell. I was casually glancing through a newsmagazine and lingered too long on a revealing photograph. By the third look, I had taken the first "drink"—the lust look—and what the alcoholics said would happen, happened. The first drink got me drunk. Within a matter of hours I was out on the streets again, having lost control, trying desperately to score.

This precipitated a lust-sex binge that lasted on and off for some three months. It was sheer hell. During that time I more than made up for the year and a half of abstinence, and wound up in "pitiful and incomprehensible demoralization," a phrase the alcoholics coined. I had become willing to throw marriage and career to the winds and be a pimp in order to supply myself with the prostitutes I wanted, and even then, I knew that would not satisfy. The marriage was over; I was living in the garage; and I was getting suicidal. I had "hit my bottom." It was the end of the line. The party was over.

Somehow, by what had to be another miracle, I was able to crawl, raving, back to AA and start all over again. But this time, I would have to *work* those Twelve Steps to survive. I got a sponsor (a friend on the program to help me work the Steps) and began working on *me*.

I started from the beginning. Step One was taken when I realized at depth that I was absolutely powerless over lust and my sex life and emotions were unmanageable. Step Two became a reality when I came slowly to believe that a power greater than myself could restore me to sanity. This came about as I re-established my connection with the Twelve Step fellowship.

With no more resorting to "drugs" to avoid the reality of my own emotions, I began to see and feel them. Raw nerve endings of resentment, negativism, anxiety, and fear became exposed. Above all, I think I was afraid of finding out what I was really like on the inside. It wasn't pretty. I discovered that uninsulated by lust, sex, pills, alcohol, or entertainment, I was a very marginal person and would have to begin growing where I had left off at the age of eight. And so the pain began. That's when I saw the truth of another paradox: We have to suffer to get well.

Working the Steps

The pain of awareness of who I really was drove me to work the Twelve Steps of recovery. The real freedom began when I could be free of my past. I became as a child, teachable, having to reject my way of doing and thinking for a new way of life based on surrender of my will to God. Then I began working on my defects, as they were uncovered not only in the inventory of my past, but in the continuing pain of seeing myself trying to relate to others. This process, of course, is still going on. I also began clearing away the wreckage of my past and making amends whenever I was wrong. Believe me, none of this came easy! I just discovered that I had to do it to survive! I had to die to myself in order to live. Another paradox.

Early in 1979, after a few hopeful beginnings that failed, Sexaholics Anonymous came into being, and since then I've been part of this fellowship of recovering sexaholics. I like what I'm doing to myself today. I don't have escape fantasies of being in a prison or leper colony anymore. The obsession and compulsion of sexual lust are gone; I've been set free. Not cured. I'm still a sexaholic; my programming still makes me want to turn my head at anything that looks interesting and take a "drink." Part of me still thinks it will die if I don't. But one day at a time, one encounter at a time, one glance at a time, one thought or memory at a time, I don't have to act on those impulses. I don't have to drink it in.

My continuing freedom is based on my attitude; if it isn't open to the grace of God and others I'm in big trouble. I can take that first drink again any time I want, inside my head, without so much as batting an eyelash! That's why my continued sobriety is predicated on maintaining a spiritual program—right attitudes about others and myself.

Healing in my marriage and in the family is one of the most blessed areas of this new life, even though things aren't always a bed of roses. I've found something better than lust—reality. But I have to be willing to give up any thought of changing partners, either actually or in fantasy, even if it means not having sex at all. Each time, I have to surrender my right to sex and depend on the grace of God. What else can you call it? And there are times my wife and I have gone without sex for extended periods. But it's all right; sex is optional now. I have a choice. And mutually voluntary periods of abstinence for a year or so have proven to be the most constructive—and happy—times of our entire marriage. For me the key was finally giving up all expectation of either sex or affection, and working on myself and my defective relations with others.

It has been a totally new beginning for us. I'm just starting to get acquainted with my wife of seventeen years. I discover to my delight she's a person: unique, independent, an individual, a whole universe of personality I was blind to before. And the more I die to any thought of resorting to someone else and commit myself to this one union, the more pleasure and love and freedom I find.

I can't believe that the person I'm writing about today is the same one who used to think and do the things I've been describing. Actually, that other person was a slave; he was living in a world of fantasy and illusion, only for himself, and always alone. He had never matured through emotional adolescence and was spiritually dead. He could not cope either with his own emotions or with life in the big world out there, and was constantly running. Running to satisfy demands and lusts that could never be satisfied. Running from who he really was; running from others; running from life; running from God, the source of his life.

The running is over. I've found what I was really looking for.

PART I

Sexaholism—The Addiction
Lust—The Force Behind the Addiction
The Spiritual Basis of Addiction

The Problem

For the sexaholic, the progression is relentless and inevitable. Within any given moment of our lives, however, we were unaware of the extent it had driven us and refused to see where it was leading. Like revelers riding a raft down the river of pleasure, we were unaware of the awesome power of the rapids or the whirlpool ahead.

First addicts, then love cripples, we took from others to fill up what was lacking in ourselves. Conning ourselves time and again that the next one would save us, we were really losing our lives.

Sexaholism— The Addiction

We sexaholics do not presume to be authorities on addiction of any kind, much less sex addiction. The trend of research on the subject reveals that the concept of what constitutes addiction is undergoing a process of evolution. Some researchers even confess to being baffled by what addiction really is. It seems the more we know, the more there is to know. We need to have some humility here. Looking at our sexaholism in terms of addiction seems to be a useful way to begin looking at ourselves.

We speak from our own experience as seen through recovery. We feel that only such an in-depth revelation will expose our condition for what it is and facilitate recovery.

Living inside our illness, we were blind to it. In recovery, the addiction begins to lose its hold over us, but it is necessary that we never forget what we really are. Had we seen but a little of this, it might have saved us years of agony and inflicting our madness on others. If we can help other sexaholics understand the true nature of what they are doing to themselves and others and encourage them to join in a fellowship of recovery before their malady reaches the malignant stage it did with many of us, we will indeed be grateful.

General Aspects of the Addiction

Our experiences have revealed three aspects of our condition that commonly identify addictions: tolerance, abstinence, and withdrawal. If someone has experienced these three phenomena in some area of his or her life, that person is generally regarded as being addicted. When we apply this test to ourselves, we identify as being addicted to lust, sex, relationships, or various combinations of these—for starters.

Tolerance

The term *tolerance* refers to the tendency to tolerate more of the drug or activity and get less from its use, hence the need for increasing dosage to maintain or recapture the desired effect. With addictions other than drugs, tolerance refers to a need for increasing amounts of obsessive thinking, interaction, or activity, with less and less effect. In short, we resort to the drug more, with diminishing satisfaction. We see how this applies in our case when we remember how our lust or sexual activity escalated over the years, crossing one line after another, first in our thought life, then in our behavior. For example, those early masturbatory fantasies were seldom enough; we graduated to seeking increasingly potent varieties. And if we got hooked on pictures, we found ourselves seeking ever-more-explicit images to use. If we began by dating for romance, it often escalated into seeking more promiscuous liaisons. Exposing ourselves in fantasy progressed to doing it in public. We needed more and more of our "drug."

Abstinence

The term *abstinence* refers to the phenomenon where the typical addict tries to quit using the addictive agent or activity. Perhaps we should call it *attempted abstinence*. We swear off—again and again. Something inside tells us we should stop. How many times did we say we *had* to stop? How many times did we actually try stopping? Some of us "stopped" every time we acted out!

Withdrawal

The term *withdrawal* is applied to the symptoms the addict may experience when deprived of the drug or activity. Such symptoms can be physical, emotional, or both. This gives rise to the deception and demand that we've *got* to have sex. But this is no different from the drug addict feeling he'll die without his fix. It is simply not true; not feeding the hunger doesn't kill us.

Some of us look back on our transition to sobriety as a time when we were in a state of shock, in which our whole system had to slowly recover from the trauma of a lifetime of self-inflicted injury. Sobriety involves a new and unfamiliar way of life, like driving in a foreign country without knowing the language or customs. Only this is a whole new *inner* terrain. Without the drug, we begin to feel what's really going on inside. It takes time to adjust to all this, and the support of others in the fellowship is vital. Journeying this new road together helps take the fear out of withdrawal. We see that others who have gone before us have discovered that sex is truly optional, *once they surrendered lust and the expectation of sex*. And their comfort and joy are genuine; they are neither abnormal nor deprived. Married members discover they can go into periods of voluntary abstinence to recover from lust and find them surprisingly effective and rewarding experiences. Yes, there is life after lust! And life after sex!

We see that the practice of our addiction includes the whole range from sporadic or periodic to continuous acting out, sometimes all within the same individual. But regardless of our particular pattern, it involves the addictive elements of tolerance, abstinence, and withdrawal, though we probably are not aware of them at the time. And if we switch addictions—not uncommon for those trying to quit one—the addictive process is the same.

Three additional aspects of our addiction we should look at are toxicity, adverse physical and emotional effects, and trigger mechanisms.

Toxicity

Toxic reactions to alcohol and drug abuse are common knowledge. What we might call the *toxicity* of lust becomes especially apparent to us in recovery. We become increasingly aware of the poisonous effects of lust on our thinking and behavior. We have heard members say, "I'm allergic to lust," and we know the person is trying to describe the toxic reaction that occurs whenever he or she takes a visual or fantasy "drink" without even acting out. In sobriety, once we have withdrawn from lust and then let it back in, the toxic effect is felt immediately and strongly. We can tolerate less of it than ever, and it produces a greater disturbance. Our sexaholism doesn't stand still; it progressively worsens.

> *"I could see a girl in a bikini on a billboard five years ago and it wouldn't bother me; now, I go to pieces and lose my mind over it."*
>
> *"Lust throws my whole system out of whack. I lose my equilibrium, my control, and have to recover as if from a poison."*

[Note: These and other italicized quotes are from Sexaholics Anonymous members, past and present.]

Adverse Physical and Emotional Effects

Who can say what is the full range of side effects that lust, sex, or relationship addiction can precipitate? We're still learning. Obvious effects are any of the proliferating horde of venereal diseases. Many of us found that impotence or frigidity also resulted from our sexaholism. But a vast range of other effects that we are just beginning to recognize accompanied many of us on our disastrous path toward sexual and emotional ruin: self-obsession; self-hatred; self-punishment; anger; loss of emotional control; isolation; and diminished ability to relate to others, concentrate, and function. Our sexaholism opened the door to a host of mental, emotional, and spiritual disorders that followed the advancing addiction.

It's as though at certain stages, our entire system cries out: Stop! You're killing me! Sexual sobriety opens the door to recovery, where the healing begins. We feel better physically, emotionally, and spiritually when sober and when the principles of the Steps are effective in our everyday lives.

Trigger Mechanisms

In our addiction we develop a growing number of *trigger mechanisms* that help set us off. These include stimuli, conflicts, or pressures that provoke a fantasy, feeling, or thought that leads to our acting out. We seem to have no trouble identifying some of our more tangible lust and sex triggers. By the time we've become addicted, we've created a whole universe of them, which expands as the addiction progresses. Here are some categories suggested from our experience; the list will never be complete.

Sex Objects. Persons of the same or opposite sex, including our own bodies. Almost anything about them can serve as triggers: various body parts, items or styles of clothing, body language, and endless varieties of speech, behavior, or attitude. Some of us include in this category animals and inanimate objects.

Media. Pictures, printed matter, ads, television and movies, music, and dance. Various places, from bars and dance halls to the streets, marketplaces, and showplaces of the city may also be considered media in the sense of what they communicate to us.

The Inner Landscape. Most of us can see how memories and fantasies can act as triggers. Intangibles we are likely to identify on our own are such things as failure, rejection, or criticism. More remotely identifiable triggers are such things as feelings of loneliness, alienation, world-weariness, boredom, isolation, "the lonely crowd," and other manifestations of unfulfilled God-hunger. Also, nudging us to reach for our drug are such things as a heightened state due to anything from compulsive work, anger, resentment, anxiety, fear, excitement, or haste, to such things as stimulating foods or beverages or even intellectual or aesthetic excitement. What we seem to be discovering is that just about anything can become a trigger, indicating that there's an underlying pathology driving our thinking and behavior. This can help us see how the whole person must be involved in recovery. Recognizing and accepting our limitations thus become crucial to recovery.

Susceptibility to such triggers is one factor behind our use of the program slogan HALT—Don't get too **H**ungry, **A**ngry, **L**onely, or **T**ired.

> **H**ungry. With many of us, an agitated state of mind—haste, hurry, or "hyper," for example—seems at least as perilous as hunger. And hunger itself can lead to binge eating, as many of us so well know. Binging on food can trigger the sexual addiction.
>
> **A**ngry. Anger, resentment, and negative thoughts toward ourselves or others create the inner disturbance that isolates us and sets us up for our drugs.
>
> **L**onely. The "unconnected" sexaholic is a *mis*connection waiting to happen.
>
> **T**ired. Fatigue often seems to make us more liable to temptation, lowering our defenses somehow, as though becoming weak physically affects our emotional stamina.

As we learn to recognize and surrender our triggers in sobriety and accept our limitations, fear of falling lessens. We learn the difference between indulging ourselves and taking care of ourselves. The new way of life works—

if, that is, we begin finding what our lust was really looking for. Finding this is the result of a patient working of the Twelve Steps, which we shall get into in Part II. Before we do so, however, it may help to review the addictive process and consider both the concept of lust and the spiritual basis of addiction.

The Addictive Process

Here again, our experiences in recovery reveal aspects of the process common to other addictions. In the early formative stages we have an overpowering desire—Is it really a demand?—for an action, interaction, or fantasy that produces a high—something to get us out of ourselves. It brings relief and pleasure, so we seek it repeatedly and compulsively. At first, it's a pleasurable way to cope with our inner conflict or stress or pain that seems intolerable. It works. Typically, sex with ourselves or others starts us off, and just as in other addictions, it dissolves tension, relieves depression, resolves conflicts or provides the means to cope with a difficult life situation or take an action that seemed impossible before. Whatever form our sexaholism takes, it has the *apparent* effect of reducing isolation; easing lack of emotion, loneliness, and tension; and of gaining power or providing escape.

This new-found "friend" not only seems to reduce our inner conflict, boredom, and negative emotions, but also offers us fusion, validation, and a false sense of aliveness. As a matter of fact, *all* of these effects are false or at best only temporary. What seems to promise life is really taking away our lives.

It is almost impossible to pinpoint exactly when, how, or why our practice becomes addictive. Eventually, the process takes on a life of its own, often unrelated to the initial causes. And unlike normal coping practices, our addictive thinking and behavior become excessive and repetitive and are forced to serve a whole lot of other functions they weren't meant to serve.

Over time, the sense of pleasure begins to diminish; we feel less relief. The habit starts producing pain, and hangover symptoms begin appearing when the pleasure is outweighed by the pain: tension, depression, rage, guilt, and even physical distress. To relieve this pain, we resort to our habit again. As we constantly call on our addictive act for instant relief, our emotional control declines. We can go into impulsive behavior and mood swings, of which we are often unaware. Intimate and social relationships deteriorate.

Some persons coming into Sexaholics Anonymous seem to be in this transition zone between pleasure and pain. Thus, they go in and out of sobriety or the Program, feeling confused about their false start.

Eventually, what we're doing disrupts our ability for daily living. The addictive patterns lower our level of consciousness and remove us from life's mainstream. We are driven to spend more time thinking about and carrying out our addiction. At the same time, we deny the addiction to avoid the pain of recognizing how much of our life it has invaded and controls. The adverse side effects produced within us become more and more damaging.

Denial becomes woven into the fabric of our being. By refusing to listen to that still small voice within, we begin by denying we are hurting ourselves. For this lie to persist, denial must pervert the reality of ourselves and others and turns into blindness. We become unwilling and finally unable to see the truth about ourselves.

Finally, our addiction takes priority over everything else, and our ability to work, live in the real world, and relate comfortably with others suffers accordingly. In advanced stages, sexaholic practice becomes our main coping mechanism and only source of pleasure. Then it no longer helps us cope and begins causing new problems that must be coped with. In this vicious cycle, what was used as the cure becomes the sickness; what was used as the medicine becomes the poison; the Answer becomes the Problem.

Summary of the Addictive Process:

It begins with an overpowering desire for a high, relief, pleasure, or escape.

It provides satisfaction.

It is sought repeatedly and compulsively.

It then takes on a life of its own.

It becomes excessive.

Satisfaction diminishes.

Distress is produced.

Emotional control decreases.

Ability to relate deteriorates.

Ability for daily living is disrupted.

Denial becomes necessary.

It takes priority over everything else.

It becomes the main coping mechanism.

The coping mechanism stops working.

The party is over.

For the sexaholic, the progression is relentless and inevitable. Within any given moment of our lives, however, we were unaware of the extent it had driven us and refused to see where it was leading. Like revelers riding a raft down the river of pleasure, we were unaware of the awesome power of the rapids or the whirlpool ahead.

Lust—The Force Behind the Addiction

What's So Wrong with Sex?

We hear this question often, and it was one of our favorite expressions of denial that we had a problem. We could ask similar questions for other addictions, the workaholic, for example. What's so wrong with honest labor? Or with compulsive overeating: What's wrong with it? We have to eat to live! Or with use of alcohol and drugs: What's wrong with a little help to relax and escape? And finally, with the sexaholic: What's so wrong with sex? It's God-given! People ask similar questions about the use of television, movies, music, etc. Usually those of us trying to rationalize our addictions are the ones coming up with these responses. When the questions are asked in such a manner, it is easy to see how we can be so misled. And sex, perhaps, carries the most confusion.

We find it confusing and difficult, if not impossible, to see the physical manifestations of our addiction as cause enough for surrender. Knowing we must stop, we go to great lengths to find reasons for quitting:

> *"I might get VD, or the wife will leave me."*
>
> *"I'll have a heart attack if I keep on eating like this."*

> *"I just* know *this weed'll give me cancer sooner or later."*
>
> *"I'll wind up with hypertension if I keep on working like this."*
>
> *"I'll get cirrhosis of the liver and brain damage if I don't stop drinking."*
>
> *"If I don't unglue myself from this Tube I'm going to turn into a vegetable."*

Such reasons are seldom enough to make the true addict stop because they deal only with externals. The clue here is that we must differentiate between the physical action and the spiritual action (attitude) taking place at the same time in the same individual. Because he lives inside his attitudes, the individual doesn't see them; *he sees only the physical activity and thinks he's feeling guilty for that.* It is truly puzzling to him. Hence the confusion on the proper motivation for wanting to stop any given addiction. When we look only at the activity itself, most of us find no sufficient motive to stop, but if we can see its spiritual consequences, this can help us despair of it sooner and surrender. Thus, we must look behind the physical to see what's really at work in our sexaholism. But first, let's take a look at lust, for it is this concept that serves as a bridge between the physical and the spiritual aspects of our sexaholism.

Lust

Why in Step One do we say we are powerless over *lust* instead of *sex*? Is not some form of sex what we are addicted to? Yes, we answer, but our problem is not simply sex, just as in compulsive overeating the problem is not simply food. Eating and sex are natural functions; the real problem in both of these addictions seems to be what we call *lust—an attitude demanding that a natural instinct serve unnatural desires.*

When we try to use food or sex to reduce isolation, loneliness, insecurity, fear, tension, or to cover our emotions, make us feel alive, help us escape, or satisfy our God-hunger, we create an unnatural appetite that misuses and abuses the natural instinct. It is not only more intense than the natural but becomes something totally different. Eating and sex enter a different dimension; they possess an unnatural spiritual component.

The addiction is thus to lust and not merely to the substance or physical act. *Lust—the attitude itself—becomes the controlling factor in the addiction.*

This may be why people exhibit lust in more than one area. Often, those of us addicted to substances or forms of behavior discover we are also addicted to negative attitudes and emotions.

> *"I remember that when I came off lust, alcohol, and tranquilizers, resentment burst forth like a dammed-up volcano. I remember thinking that controlling lust must be like trying to control a piece of jello; you press in here and it bulges out there. Or like trying to rout a gopher; you plug up one tunnel only to have the beast go to work in another."*

People may not be allergic to food and sex in the sense some people are allergic to pollen, strawberries, or cats, but we do become "allergic" to *lust* for food and sex. Misusing the natural instinct of sex for an unnatural end over and over again increasingly sensitizes us to the triggers of that association, until a simple thought or look elicits the compulsion.

For the sexaholic, lust is toxic. This is why in recovery, the real problem is spiritual and not merely physical. This is why change of attitude is so crucial.

What Is Lust?

A Personal Point of View

It's pretty tough to get a handle on it, but here's what lust looks like in my life. It's a slave master that wants to control my sex for its own ends in its own way whenever it wants. And it's like mental-spiritual noise that distorts and perverts sex, much as a raucous radio interference distorts a lovely melody.

Lust is not sex, and it is not physical. It seems to be a screen of self-indulgent fantasy separating me from reality—either the reality of my own person in sex with myself or the reality of my spouse. It works the same way whether with a girlfriend, a prostitute, or my wife. It thus negates identity, either mine or the other person's, and is anti-real, working against my own reality, *working against me.*

I can't have true union with my wife while lust is active because she as a person really doesn't matter; she's even in the way; she's merely the sexual instrument. And I can't have true union within myself while I'm splitting myself having sex with myself. That fantasy partner I've conjured up in my mind is really part of *me*! With lust, the sex act is not the *result* of personal union; sex doesn't flow from that union. Sex energized by lust makes true union impossible.

The nature of the lust-noise interference I superimpose over sex can be many things: memories, fantasies ranging from the erotic to revenge or even violence. Or, it can be the mental image of a single fetish or of some other person. Seen in this light, lust can exist apart from sex. Indeed, there are those who say they are obsessed with lust who can no longer have sex. I see my lust as a force that apparently infuses and distorts my other instincts as well: eating, drinking, working, anger. . . . I *know* I have a lust to resent; it seems as strong as sexual lust ever was.

In my experience, lust is not physical; it is not even strong sexual desire. It seems to be a spiritual force that distorts my instincts; and whenever let loose in one area, seems to want to infect other areas as well. And being nonsexual, lust crosses all lines, including gender. When energized by lust, my sexual fantasies or acting out can go in any direction, shaped by whatever I experience. Thus, the more I indulge in sexual lust, the less truly sexual I become.

Therefore, my basic problem as a recovering sexaholic is to live free from my lust. When I entertain it in any form, sooner or later it tries to express itself in every form. And lust becomes the indicator of not only what I do, but what I am.

But there is great hope here. By surrendering lust and its acting out each time I'm tempted by it, and then experiencing God's life-giving deliverance from its power, recovery and healing are taking place, and wholeness is being restored—true union within myself first, then with others and the Source of my life.

Lust Is . . .

Not being able to say no
Constantly being in dangerous sexual situations
Turning my head as if sex-starved all the time
Attraction only to beautiful people
Erotic fantasies
Use of erotic media
Being addicted to the partner as I would be to a drug
Losing my identity in the partner
Obsession with the romantic—going for the "chemistry"
The desire to make the other person lust

Another Personal Perspective

Lust Kills

Lust is the most important thing in my life; it takes priority over *me*.
Captive to lust, I cannot be *myself*.
Lust makes me its slave; it kills my freedom; it kills *me*.

Lust always wants more; lust creates more lust.
Lust is jealous; it wants to possess me.
Lust makes me self-obsessed; it drives me into myself.

Lust makes sex impossible without lust.
Lust destroys the ability to love; it kills love.
Lust destroys the ability to receive love; it kills *me*.

Lust creates guilt—unavoidably; and guilt has to be expiated.
Lust makes part of me want to die because I can't bear what I'm doing to myself and my powerlessness over it.
Increasingly, I direct this guilt and self-hatred inward and outward.
Lust is destructive to me and those around me.

Lust kills the spirit; my spirit is me. Lust kills *me*!

The Spiritual Basis of Addiction

The physical and psychological aspects of the addictive process are becoming increasingly identifiable, and sexaholism shares elements in common with other addictions. Our sexual experience or fantasy usually began as "the answer" to all our needs. It worked. It provided relief and pleasure like nothing else. At some point, most of us came to qualify on all counts as true addicts, and some of us were probably addicted from the very beginning.

In looking back, many of us see that regardless of how, why, or when it began, there came a time when we were not only aware of the power this thing held over us, but that we were acting *against our wills*. Only when we tried stopping did we see that we were captive to a force stronger than we, at the mercy of a power greater than ourselves. We could understand the dilemma of some professionals who had tried treating alcoholics (and some of us!) only to despair.

In recovery, we came to see aspects of our sexaholism lying behind the physical and psychological that paralleled similar aspects discovered by recovering alcoholics. These have to do with the personality, dealing with the will and the attitudinal forces shaping the person and character. We refer to this as the *spiritual* dimension. It is here where we discover the most powerful forces propelling us into our addiction.

Thus, we will use the word *spiritual* in referring to that aspect of ourselves underlying and determining all our attitudes, choices, thoughts, and behavior—the very core of personality, the very heart of the person. If we can see how the addictive process involves this most fundamental aspect of our being, we will be able to understand why recovery—whatever else we make it—must be a spiritual process.

We use the term *spiritual* in this broader, nonreligious sense for another reason. Some of us testify to having led a spiritual life while still practicing our wrongs. Now we see that the spiritual realm encompasses both good and evil, and that regardless of our spiritual experiences—real though they may have been—what we were doing was neither good nor right.

Origins

Perhaps the best way to illustrate the spiritual perspective is to use a personal story. The following is an excerpt from a Fourth Step inventory written by a recovering sexaholic. (This was part of his second Fourth Step, written after a few years in recovery.)

> When I told mother about my first masturbation, she told me not to touch myself and to never bring it up again. Of course, she didn't handle the situation right, but that's where I seem to connect with the wrong in me.
>
> I closed off inside, like dropping a curtain between me and her—and the world too, somehow. I threw

some kind of tremendous silent switch. I would never again be on the outside what I was on the inside. What I was on the inside suddenly changed, and part of me retreated into that dark tunnel, way inside myself. I think that's when my resentment must have crystallized inside me. Let me see if I can play it back.

I remember turning away from my mother, silently submissive on the outside, but something on the inside turned deep and dark. I just know I had a drastic change of attitude then, like a whole new mode of being. I was going to do what I wanted to do!

This attitude was *against* my mother. In order for me to keep doing what I wanted, I had to set myself against her. But it had to be on the inside, because I was afraid to assert myself.

There wasn't even a dilemma; I just went ahead and masturbated again without a thought. But every time thereafter, masturbation had a totally new feeling to it. It got me out of myself. A vast satisfaction. Great relief. Total escape from that inner pressure. What fantastic release!

As a matter of fact, the first and subsequent masturbations seemed like totally different experiences. The first was simply a new and pleasurable physical sensation that I didn't understand and something I could bring out and discuss. The others weren't really physical at all; masturbation was merely the means for entering a whole new and free world inside me. It was spiritual, there's no other way to describe it. I really can't overstate this feeling. The physical was nice but no big deal; but what a glorious discovery the other was!

Let's see if we can dissect this sample of experience, isolating it from the sexual activity, to see if we can discern a spiritual process at work in the development of addiction.

- Based on a real or imagined injury, we create and hold on to a wrong toward another; we choose to distort the truth. Rebellion and hence resentment are born. (Perhaps a more inclusive term, *sin*, would be more appropriate.)
- This distortion of reality produces a false spiritual high—satisfaction, pleasure, and release from the conflict produced by our wrong. Rebellion and resentment fill a need (really a demand).
- We take nourishment from the resentment; it sustains us. It sustains the new reality, which is a lie. It hides our wrong; we don't have to face it and deal with it. Thus, resentment is used as a drug.
- To continue justifying this wrong to ourselves, we periodically play the incident back, winning the case in court against the other person every time. By thus reexperiencing the resentment, we seek to recapture the effect of the original high.
- Our use of resentment thus becomes habitual, producing more wrong, which requires more of the drug to cover it. The vicious cycle is set; it has a life of its own, unrelated to the initial event.
- Persistence in this habit produces distress. Part of us always knows when we're wrong: the lie doesn't square with something inside us, with what we see in the real world outside, and with inputs we get from others. Plus, we feel guilty for enjoying this unnatural ecstasy, and our isolation increases.
- We try abstaining from this inner spiritual habit, so we act outwardly toward the objects of our resentment as though we hold no wrong against them. But this pretense deprives us of our drug (resentment), creates a new lie that needs more drug, and forces us to treat the distress of withdrawal with the medicine that provides relief—more resentment.

- This mental behavior fulfills the three criteria of addiction noted earlier: tolerance, abstinence, and withdrawal. *We are now fully addicted to resentment as a spiritual attitude,* quite apart from any physical acting-out.

Now, if we add the ingredient of some physical habit to this spiritual-mental process, as we do in our case with sex, we can see how the imprinting, conditioning, and programming become all the more total, rigid, and controlling. Once this pattern is established in the disposition of the inner person, it *must* manifest itself in some form of overt behavior—we are addicts waiting to happen. Thus, the addictive *process* may be established in the inner person long before it ever appears in our behavior.

When the man described above withdrew from his lust and sex addiction, resentment, which he had never before been aware of, suddenly erupted with volcanic fury and possessed him as lust had done previously. His physical addiction had been used to cover or drug the spiritual illness. For there to be any true and lasting recovery for him, he must right the wrongs in his life from the inside out. To stay sober sexually and grow in recovery, he will have to surrender his resentments.

The Spiritual Process

From the preceding example and what we know from the experiences of other recovering sexaholics, let us summarize the elements of the spiritual process underlying and fueling the addictive process. As we take up each of these in turn, we will see by the end of each point that *we* are responsible in each stage of the process. Regardless of other factors contributing to our addiction, *we* are the active agent in its development.

An Attitude Change

A change of attitude sets the course for our addiction. It is nothing less than a change of heart. It may take place suddenly or slowly, over time. And it can happen at any time, though usually very early, in childhood or adolescence. In many of us, our sexual misbehavior seems to have been the focal point for rebellion against authority. Under the surface, many a sexaholic is seething with resentment, hostility, anger, envy, rebellion, and rage. We may not be consciously aware of it or of the powerful life-altering significance of such a disposition, but the more we discover about this aspect of our condition, the more we realize that our behavior was the manifestation of inner attitudes and thoughts. To put it another way, our attitudes enabled the addiction. External conditions did not really make us what we are. Our attitude *toward* those conditions shaped our response. Attitude transcends the externals; attitude makes the person. We are what we think.

Thus, we create our own predisposition to addiction.

A Decision to Persist in Wrong

The attitude change produces a decision to persist in doing something wrong. There is probably no such thing as an attitude change in the abstract; it is usually tied in with another person. It sets us against another. Focusing on some real or imagined wrong, we choose to resent that person, do what we want, and push the person away. We may still be dependent on them, as with a parent, brother, sister, or spouse, but we separate from them in our heart. *A wrong attitude toward others is the key to the negative spiritual process empowering the addiction.*

The missing link between the original attitude change and the subsequent addiction is that *the wrong attitude itself becomes an addiction.* We nourish, defend, and deny it.

> *"I know I get a 'hit' off that resentment every time I play back the scene with that person in my mind. It's like taking a drink from something deep inside me. Why? What's it doing for me? At times I swear I'm hooked on resentment more than I ever was on lust or alcohol!"*

Resentment is said to be the number one killer of addicts. We will have to start undoing our addiction from the inside out.

Thus, our wrongs hold us in bondage; we sin against ourselves.

Guilt and Punishment

Unknown to ourselves, we thus reap the penalty for everything we think and do wrong. For every wrong, there is a reaction within us that negates life, adding to the pool of our emotional and spiritual distress.

> *"'Dear God!' I cried out that day, 'that's* me *in there! I am what I think and do—every moral choice and attitude! Once I've let anything into the Stream of my life, it's part of* me. *Coursing through my whole life. Like a contagion, every negative deed and thought seeps into that Stream, till I find myself reeking with this polluted waterway. Polluted me, polluting* me!'"

> *"I never realized that I've been dragging my entire past with me. Every one of these people are still alive in my mind, and I'm reliving every one of these incidents, whether big or small. This cancer has been eating away at me my entire life!"*

Thus, we defile and punish ourselves.

Self-Obsession

As we make the conscious spiritual choices setting into motion the addictive process, we become increasingly selfish and self-centered. A rebellious attitude sets in, with or without pseudo-compliance on the surface. In order to keep from looking at ourselves, we find fault with those closest to us as well as with the institutions ministering to our needs. All we can see are the inadequacies, wrongs, and injustices of others.

We become increasingly closed off and defensive, unteachable and willful, and a kind of hardening sets in. Obsession with self is a negative spiritual attitude and force. Though the world outside may not see it as such, our spouses, children, fellow-workers, cats, and dogs know different. Self-obsession smells bad to everyone but the obsessed.

Our self-obsession takes different forms, from one in plain view to the covered, where it is disguised under passivity and the appearance of gentleness or pseudo-concern. The greater the self-obsession, the greater the con to disguise it. It prevents us from detecting the emerging flaws that later will turn into cracks and disastrous fissures in the reservoir of the self. And self-obsession inevitably produces spiritual blindness. To keep from seeing ourselves, we seize on the wrongs of others.

Most difficult for us to see was that being obsessed with self meant we had become the Source of our own lives—our own god. *We* were the most important person in our world. Thus, we had to connect with ourselves; we became addicted to ourselves. No wonder so many of us found masturbation to be infinitely more than childhood experimentation. It got us high on ourselves, short-circuiting any meaningful connection with others and God.

In our great and lofty pursuits of "finding" our lives we shut out the possibility of ever receiving life.

> *"The program people showed it to me. I'm high on myself. I'm sitting there, talking about* myself

> *and* my *wife and* my *job and those* people *out there! And I'm the center of the universe and can't see that* that's *the problem! It got to be awful lonely, sitting on that throne of God."*

Thus, we make ourselves god.

Separation

From our very first attitude change, we isolate ourselves. We start building a wall around us, especially between us and those we are close to. It may appear that just the opposite is true. We can be outgoing, warm, personable, charming, lovable, and kind—as long as it serves the self. The reality of the matter is simply that we cannot hang on to resentments or practice our addiction without negating true union.

At the same time, we are separating ourselves from God. Our way of life sets us on a course *away from* instead of toward. And this is inevitably true, even though we may still be fervently engaging in religious exercises or having spiritual experiences or are sober in other programs.

This process has an even more insidious aspect—separation from ourselves. We start moving farther and farther away from that part of ourselves that has the light, until we may finally lose it. The duplicity of holding resentments on the inside while being something else on the outside creates a split that not only isolates us from others but from our true selves—separation at the very core of our being.

No wonder we start having so much trouble with our mental health. We push the light (truth about ourselves and others) farther and farther away until finally, when none gets through the shield of self-will, the darkness descends. The result is isolation, alienation, depression, and disunion within ourselves. Is not this an insanity all its own?

Thus, we lose ourselves.

Blindness and Delusion

As soon as we set into motion the process of covering our wrongs, there is an increasing inability to see ourselves as we really are and others as they really are. The alcoholics call this *pride-blindness.* How sharply attuned we became to the defects of others. Our ability to detect hypocrisy in others seemed to increase in direct proportion to our own self-blindness, as though we had to sharpen our critical spirit the more to keep from looking inward. Often our judgmental attitude took on great heat as we raged against people, places, and things. We could not see that we were half a dimension off, that the reality within *us* had shifted. We would never know the real truth about ourselves or others until we had a change of heart.

We were particularly blind to the perception of our addiction. Even though part of us knew the habit controlled us, it was often the one thing in our lives we thought we were controlling. This made letting go of the habit more difficult.

The blindness starts as we deny the truth about our wrongs and hold on to the lie of our own rationalizations. Reality gets turned upside down. What is wrong becomes right because we're doing it. Self-obsession at work! This creates willful blindness—delusion—for which there is no cure except a change of heart.

> *"Well, I stepped out on the wife again last night. But you know, it really didn't bother me as much this time; I didn't feel guilty. I simply won't let it affect our relationship. I couldn't do that. And as long as she doesn't know. . . "*

The deterioration goes ever inward. Thus, many of us appeared to be normal, healthy specimens, with simply an emotional problem or two. We even fooled the professionals. No wonder so many of us thought of suicide. The gnawing realization of dying on the inside left us with nothing to resort to but more of the same sick thinking and behavior.

Not even the threat of untreatable venereal disease could induce us to forsake our habit. (Some of us called it "LOVE.") It wasn't unusual for us to feel miraculously exempt from all judgment, even divinely protected.

Thus, we delude ourselves.

The Negative Connection

We find that spiritual isolation is intolerable for long. Nature abhors a vacuum. Self-obsession tries to fill this void, since it is a closed-loop connection with the self. Another substitute connection within ourselves was masturbation, which often continued through marriage and other relationships as the "normal" experience.

But our mis-connection went deeper. It seems that with all our human drives—hunger, thirst, sex, power, and the like—the most basic is what we might call the Person-drive, the drive to have union with another. This drive *must* have its Connection. Without this essential core of our being plugged in somewhere, life is unbearable. We can't just leave the plug of our soul dangling. We can't survive alone, cut off, disconnected. But most of us confused the personal with the sexual, as though only the sexual aspect of this union would satisfy what essentially is a spiritual drive. So, we used sex or lust or relationships to satisfy this drive, letting them take the place of God *as source of our lives.* Idolatry.

This negative connection never satisfies. The hunger merely deepens, and the compulsive pursuit of *more* and *different* and *better* accelerates. Just as the Person-drive is the force driving us to connect with the best in us, others, and God, lust becomes the negative force connecting us with the worst in us and others and with what someone has called our negative god. It is in this area where some recovering members see in their sexaholism an aspect they call the diabolical.

Thus, we pervert ourselves.

Spiritual Death

When we look at these spiritual aspects of the addictive process, we are forced to face some things we simply could not accept before we surrendered. Prior to our recovery, it was impossible for any of us to comprehend or accept the true nature of our condition. "Sure," we said, "there must be some poor sex drunks who are that bad off, but not me!" Looking deeper, we said, "Yes, me!"

We choose the course that sets us against ourselves and others so we can persist in wrong. Self-obsession is a spiritual delirium all its own, an idolatry of the most insidious sort. Our diseased attitude is an irresistible force driving us away from others, ourselves, and God and into our addictions. The darker side of our negative connection is truly fearsome. And the insanity of our delusion damns us to a condition where truth about ourselves cannot penetrate. We must finally ask, then, Doesn't all this add up to spiritual death?

The stakes are higher than we figured. Had we ever glimpsed the truth for a moment, the torment would have been greater than we could bear. Thus, the illness *must* perpetuate itself, both within and without. To stop means we must face the truth about ourselves, and that is like the very threat of death. But unless we do stop and face the truth about ourselves, we remain in death.

Thus, we destroy ourselves.

Conclusions

When we look at the addictive process, we see that what we call the spiritual factors lie beneath the psychological and behavioral. This underlying soul sickness, now apparent to us only in recovery, is the root of our problem. We are forced to certain conclusions: (1) Sexaholism is an addiction, and we sexaholics have the same basic characteristics as any other addicts, and perhaps some unique ones of our own. (2) The nature of what we have been doing to ourselves is truly shattering. (3) Our addiction is an inside job; *we* are responsible for the attitudes that set its course and propel our thinking and behavior. (4) *Since we had something to do with becoming what we are, we can assume responsibility for the change of attitude—surrender—that will allow healing to begin.* We can become willing to see and surrender what we know we're doing wrong. The Fellowship and the Program of the Steps take it from there.

Every time we "go back out there"—our way of saying we have resorted to our addiction once again—we set in motion these same self-destructive processes. We start another countdown that leads to an end that progressively worsens. There's no way we can avoid restarting the self-destruct mechanism, and no knowing when we will reach that point of no return.

If all of this leaves you with a feeling of despair, that very despair may indicate you are willing to face the truth about yourself for the first time. It was to such despair that we had to come before we could be released. Left to our own devices, the prognosis is dismal. Only for those who want recovery is there any hope at all, and to such, we offer great hope: release from the power of addiction, loss of guilt and shame, power over wrong and freedom to do right, and the ability to live comfortably with ourselves, others, and God. This is precisely what the Fellowship of the Steps will do when we make it a way of life.

But the hope we offer lies in a certain direction. Since sexaholism is essentially a spiritual process in its origin and development, it follows that the program of recovery giving us the best results is also essentially spiritual. Since our condition is characterized by the relentless progression of diseased attitudes, recovery for us lies in a profound change of attitude toward ourselves, others, and God, and in the righting of our wrongs. Thus, SA is a program of action, from the inside out.

You don't have to understand any of this to recover. If it has parted the veil of obscurity and misinformation cloaking our condition for only a brief glimpse inside, it will have served its purpose. It should also help those of us in recovery to understand the radical nature of the change of heart and character that must continue if we are to live sober, joyous, and free.

A Note on Use of the Term "Spiritual." We quote from Appendix II of *Alcoholics Anonymous*:

> The terms *spiritual experience* and *spiritual awakening* are used many times in this book which, upon careful reading, shows that the personality change sufficient to bring about recovery from alcoholism has manifested itself among us in many different forms. . . .
>
> Most of our experiences are [of]. . .the "educational variety" because they develop slowly over a period of time. Quite often friends of the newcomer are aware of the difference long before he is himself. He finally realizes that he has undergone a profound alteration in his reaction to life; that such a change could hardly have been brought about by himself alone. What often takes place in a few months could seldom have been accomplished by years of self-discipline. With few exceptions our members find that they have tapped an unsuspected inner resource which they presently identify with their own conception of a Power greater than themselves.
>
> Most of us think this awareness of a Power greater than ourselves is the essence of spiritual experience. Our more religious members call it "God-consciousness."
>
> Most emphatically we wish to say that any alcoholic capable of honestly facing his problems in the light of our experience can recover, provided he does not close his mind to all spiritual concepts. He can only be defeated by an attitude of intolerance or belligerent denial.
>
> We find that no one need have difficulty with the spirituality of the program. *Willingness, honesty and openmindedness are the essentials of recovery. But these are indispensable.*
>
> "There is a principle which is a bar against all information, which is proof against all arguments and which cannot fail to keep a man in everlasting ignorance—that principle is contempt prior to investigation." (Herbert Spencer) [From *Alcoholics Anonymous*, pp. 569–570.]

PART II

The Solution

We saw that our problem was threefold: physical, emotional, and spiritual. Healing had to come about in all three.

The crucial change in attitude began when we admitted we were powerless, that our habit had us whipped. We came to meetings and withdrew from our habit. For some, this meant no sex with themselves or others, including not getting into relationships. For others it also meant "drying out" and not having sex with the spouse for a time to recover from lust.

We discovered that we *could* stop, that not feeding the hunger didn't kill us, that sex was indeed optional. There was hope for freedom, and we began to feel alive. Encouraged to continue, we turned more and more away from our isolating obsession with sex and self and turned to God and others.

All this was scary. We couldn't see the path ahead, except that others had gone that way before. Each new step of surrender felt it would be off the edge into oblivion, but we took it. And instead of killing us, surrender was killing the obsession! We had stepped into the light, into a whole new way of life.

The fellowship gave us monitoring and support to keep us from being overwhelmed, a safe haven where we could finally face ourselves. Instead of covering our feelings with compulsive sex, we began exposing the roots of our spiritual emptiness and hunger. And the healing began.

As we faced our defects, we became willing to change; surrendering them broke the power they had over us. We began to be more comfortable with ourselves and others for the first time without our "drug."

Forgiving all who had injured us, and without injuring others, we tried to right our own wrongs. At each amends more of the dreadful load of guilt dropped from our shoulders, until we could lift our heads, look the world in the eye, and stand free.

We began practicing a positive sobriety, taking the actions of love to improve our relations with others. We were learning how to give; and the measure we gave was the measure we got back. We were finding what none of the substitutes had ever supplied. We were making the real Connection. We were home.

Getting Started

Step "Zero"

There is an unwritten step underlying all twelve. Call it Step Zero: *"We participated in the fellowship of the program."* No one seems able to stay sober and progress in recovery without it, though some try. For most of us, without associating in some way with other recovering individuals, there is no lasting sobriety and none of the fringe benefits of recovery, growth, freedom, and joy. This holds true even for "loners" (those without groups). We don't try to explain this; it is simply a fact.

We begin by meeting regularly with other members. If there is no group where we live, we start one ourselves, even if it is meeting with only one other member. Fellowship is that crucial to our recovery. We can't do it alone. We pray to be led to another sexaholic who will want to hear our story, then we follow all leads that come to our attention. We contact the SA Central Office for any contacts there may be in our area and ask for materials and know-how. (See part III and Appendix 3.) Many groups have started in just such a manner. Long distances may separate members at first; some travel more than a hundred miles to meet with others.

Commit yourself to your group, whether it is being formed or is operating but still small. Attend every meeting on time. This ensures maximum benefit to you and the group, which cannot have continuity without regular participants. The measure of such commitment will be the measure of your recovery.

We also use telephone meetings with two or more members, using the three-way calling feature available in many cities. Some members subscribe to discount long-distance phone service for considerable savings. Speaker phones enable a loner to sit in remotely. We augment this by letter writing and attending other types of Twelve Step meetings, many of which are open to the public. Much benefit can be gained there in learning how to apply the Steps in one's life and in seeing how meetings are run.

We cannot put this strongly enough: Experience has shown us that we must be part of others or we cannot maintain effective surrender, see ourselves rightly, or work the Steps. *Without regular participation in the fellowship, there seems to be no recovery.*

We Stop

We stop practicing our compulsion in all its forms. We can't be "sober" in one area while acting out in another. There can be no relief from the obsession of lust while still practicing the acts of lust in any form.

> *"I can be masturbating to the image of a blank wall, and I'm still resorting to my drug."*

We stop feeding lust. We get rid of all the materials and other triggers under our control. We stop feeding lust through the eyes, the fantasy, and the memory. We stop relishing the language of lust, resentment, and rage. We stop living only and always inside our own heads. One of the fringe benefits of going to a lot of meetings is that it gets us out of ourselves.

As we become aware of other addictions that are part of our lives, we pray for willingness to surrender each one.

There can be no true recovery from addiction if we allow it to persist in any area, whether in our thinking or in our acting out.

What we are really saying when we start meeting with others is, *"I have to stop; please help me."*

But we need some demonstration of trust, and hearing the stories of other members, we begin to let our guard down. Before we know it, we've crossed that line of doubt, mistrust, and fear, and have put down our drug.

The program doesn't tell us how to stop—we had done that a thousand and one times—it shows us how to keep from starting again. We had it backwards; before, we always wanted the therapist, spouse, or God to do the stopping for us—to fix us. Now, *we* stop; and *then*, in our surrender, the power of God becomes effective in us.

We Get Involved

At first, all that many of us could do was simply attend meetings. "Forget the Steps, forget everything, just bring the body," we were told. And bring the body we did, even if we had to drag it along and even if the mind and will lagged far behind. But soon, we started sharing at meetings, telling our story, bringing the inside out. And we discovered that the way to feel better is not only going to meetings but taking the risk of self-disclosure.

> *"Inside my head, those problems seemed so hopeless. Just bringing them out into the light cut them down to size."*

We followed the suggestion of getting involved in the mechanics of meetings: helping set up, cleaning up, maintaining the literature, and being there for newcomers. Involvement made us feel we were a *part of*, quite a difference from that empty, lifeless feeling of being *apart from*.

> *"Doing things—anything—got me out of myself and into the real world."*

It was from such simple beginnings that we could later feel more comfortable in meeting other members one-to-one and in going out after meetings. We began the painful but welcome process of growing up by coming out of ourselves. The fellowship of sobriety is where the action is, where the magic is, where the feeling of identification is, where the real Connection is.

We received or asked for the phone number of one or more members we could call or contact regularly. This seemed strange and unnatural to many of us, until we discovered that was how many others got help to stay sober at first.

> *"Suddenly, I was worthwhile, as sick as I was. What dignity there is in that total acceptance!"*

The First Test—Surrender

Joining a group doesn't automatically make the problem vanish. Most of us had tried stopping countless times. The problem was we couldn't stay stopped; we had never surrendered. So, the first time the craving hits again, when we get that urge for a fix, we give it up, even though it feels like we'll die without it. And at times, in our new frame of mind, the craving may seem stronger than ever. But we don't fight it like we used to; that was always a losing battle, giving it more strength to fight back. Neither do we feed or give in to it. We surrender. We win by giving up. Each time.

Coming off our habit can be confusing.

> *"My head turns automatically! I can't help feeding it. I don't have any choice!"*

But we always fed our habit. We simply weren't aware of it. So whenever this happens, we simply acknowledge our powerlessness. Instead of either fighting or indulging, we surrender. We pick up the phone, we ask for help, we go to a meeting. We even admit we may not fully want victory over lust; most of us don't have pure motives in wanting to get sober. Recovery is a slow process.

The first time we walk through the stress of withdrawal without resorting to the drug, we discover that we don't die without that fix. Instead, we feel better, stronger, that maybe there's hope. We talk about the temptation in a phone call or at the next meeting and tell all. Telling the deep truth in an attitude of surrender helps break the power the memory of the incident holds over us. And if we're hit with lust again, we keep coming back and talking it out, regardless of how shameful and defeated we feel. We've all been there; we know how it feels. We also know the release and joy that surrender brings as we come back into the light.

Usually we find that our initial surrender was incomplete and we begin to see some loose ends. We discover some rain checks secretly stashed against future need. Like alcoholics hiding their bottles.

> *"It's* her *key; I can't throw that away."*
>
> *"I'll keep his phone number; I may be able to help him sometime."*
>
> *"I'll get rid of the magazines later. . ."*

In recovery, we simply throw the stuff away. No one has to tell us, we just know. We always knew; we just never had the power to let them go.

The Next Test, and the Next . . .

Sooner or later, the urge strikes again, sometimes out of nowhere, like a tidal wave crashing over us. Wham! Maybe it's the first time we feel rejected. Any of countless triggers can do it; it really doesn't matter what they are. We all have them.

> *"It's too overpowering! . . . No one will know the difference."*
>
> *"A look never killed anyone. . ."*
>
> *"Everyone's doing it!"*
>
> *"I never thought I'd hear from him again. Now what do I do?"*

Often it begins in the privacy of our innermost thoughts, when we're alone, when we're living inside our head and the emotions we could never face overwhelm us. So what do we do? Naturally, we want to reach for the drug again; that's what we programmed ourselves to do. Instead, we surrender. Again. Just like the first time. And the cry for help goes up again: *I'm powerless; please help me!*

And we take the action of getting out of ourselves and making contact with another member. As soon as possible. The closer to the heat of the action the better. We use the phone. We make the call. Not because we want to, *because we don't want to*. We call because we know we have to. Our survival instinct comes to life. And we go to a meeting as soon as possible.

When we first come into the program, this cry for help is, in effect, a shotgun working of Steps One, Two, and Three. Surrender, of whatever sort. That's all it takes, and not one of us does it with all the right motives. When the craving hits again, we repeat this surrender at the very point of our terror, in the pit of our hell. For that's where the admission of powerlessness really works, when we're in the raw heat of temptation and craving. Again, it's the change of attitude that brings relief. Instead of, "I've got to have it or I'll die!" our attitude becomes, "I give up; I'm willing *not* to have it, even if I do die."

And we don't die! We get a reprieve. Again. For seconds, minutes, hours, perhaps even days and weeks. The tidal wave is spent. The craving passes. And we're okay. We are learning the truth of the program maxim, "One Day at a Time."

But there will be another wave behind it, and sooner or later we get hit again. This may knock us off balance.

> *"Why do I always feel recovered after each bout and then get caught off guard by the next wave?"*

Often, seeing we've stopped acting out our habit for a time, we feel we're free of it forever. This may just be the time it strikes again. So the realization slowly dawns that we may always be subject to temptation and powerless over lust. We come to see that it's all right to be tempted and feel absolutely powerless over it *as long as we can get the power to overcome.* The fear of our vulnerability gradually diminishes as we stay sober and work the Steps. We can look forward to the time when the obsession—not temptations—will be gone.

We begin to see that there's no power over the craving in advance; we have to work this *as it happens each time.* Therefore, each temptation, every time we want to give in to lust or any other negative emotion, is a gift toward recovery, healing, and freedom—another opportunity to change our attitude and find union with God. We didn't get here in a day; it took practice to burn the addictive process into our being. It takes practice to make our true Connection.

Reprieve

At the first sign of relief from the obsession, we may get complacent. Once we've learned to live without the most obvious stuff, we may sit back and relax—take it easy.

> *"It's like the switch just turned off. Sobriety's a snap; there's nothing to it."*

We may feel as though the obsession was really something foreign to us, pulled out like a thorn from a finger; that *we* can remain unchanged, with the same attitudes and thinking as before.

> *"I'll just get outta here and go see that movie. I can always close my eyes on the bad scenes."*

Like it or not, that's the way many of us seem to do it. By degrees. Instead of running joyously to heaven, we seem to back away from our hell, one step at a time. Thus, often shying away from full slips, some of us think we can allow ourselves partial slips, enjoying the temporary relief they bring. Testing our limits. We have all sorts of strategies for denial.

We may start looking around, just free enough of the compulsion to start noticing what's out there again. And we see that everyone seems to be doing what we can no longer get away with. We feel the pull of it inside.

> *"How can anything that looks and feels that good be so bad for me?"*

A sadness may come over us. We may find it hard to go to sleep. We may get fidgety, feel at a loss, feel empty, not knowing what's wrong. The old inner panic hits again, and we reach for our drug.

That's when we get into action again. The pain—not to mention the fear of falling—jolts us into reality. We go to a meeting, get on the phone, contact someone we trust. We get out of ourselves and get moving.

> *"If I stay inside my head now, I'm dead!"*

Again, we acknowledge that we are powerless over the obsession, only now we may add a little more to our cry of desperation: *"Please help me. Thy will, not mine, be done."*

And another breath of relief and comfort comes. Reprieve again. Respite. Even though we may be lulled into complacency again, this is a moment of inner peace, the likes of which we never knew before.

We can be deceived because we may have surrendered "on a full stomach." We'd just finished a destructive bout and sworn off, "Never again!" And we meant it. (Didn't we always?) But the very next time we have the urge and the wave breaks over us again knocking us off our feet, we don't act out our habit, we don't resort to our drug—one day at a time, one hour at a time, sometimes one minute at a time. And the craving passes!

Surrender is a constant thing. Practice. Day by day, hour by hour. Put into practice so often, it becomes habitual. *That's how we get the attitude change that lets the grace of God enter to expel the obsession!*

We Get a Glimpse of Ourselves

Perhaps we weather the first several waves of lust or temptation in withdrawal and then think we have it under control. Maybe we take a look in the mirror; meetings and contact with other members have a way of helping us see ourselves. We start getting insights into what the habit has been doing to us—to our bodies, emotions, ability to function, will to live, families, jobs, money, time. . . . We begin seeing things inside us that we'd been using the drug to cover over.

> *"Why can't I let go of this terrible resentment?"*
>
> *"How could I have put my wife through that agony again?"*

As dim outlines of our sick patterns emerge, we continue changing our attitudes. We start looking at ourselves. For the first time, the truth dawns on us: ". . . every time we are disturbed, no matter what the cause, there is something wrong *with us*. If somebody hurts us and we are sore, we are in the wrong also." (*Twelve Steps and Twelve Traditions*, p. 90)

We also begin to detect some of our more subtle rationalizations:

> *"I'm in the neighborhood; I'll just go by and say Hi."*
>
> *"I'll call the old relationship and tell him I'm in the program."*
>
> *"I'll just take a glance to see if it's something I shouldn't be looking at."*

We may even find ourselves cruising the old haunts or flirting—for no special reason, of course. Maybe I'll just be swept off my feet and overwhelmed, so I won't be responsible, we think. Such attitudes can persist in sobriety.

Though we keep hearing "Half measures availed us nothing," we go through the phase where they seem to avail us something. Apparently we have to see this for ourselves and at our own pace, even if we fall flat on our faces. Thus, in the flush of new-found sobriety and success, we can be setting ourselves up for a fall. Lust is cunning, baffling, and powerful—and very patient. But if we want recovery, *we keep coming back!*

This may be the time many of us start thinking seriously about what the program is all about. We may have been surviving hit-and-miss on the first part of Step One and maybe bits and pieces of a few others. But we're not going anywhere. Maybe we've even slipped and are hurting and don't know what hit us or what to do about it. Confusion and puzzlement reign.

> "*I* believe *in the Steps; what's wrong? Why isn't it working for me?*"

We're sitting there, staring into space, and it dawns on our dullness: *The Steps won't work for me unless I work them!*

Up to this point, recovery may have been just as compulsive as the addiction. But there comes a time when this isn't enough. It's just too uncomfortable. We begin to see that the obsession and compulsive acting out are only symptoms of our underlying spiritual illness. Even the fellowship isn't enough. We have to get to the source of the problem—ourselves. Instead of that subconscious and insidious attitude, "Please fix me!" as though some other person or group could do the recovery for us, *we take responsibility for our own recovery. We start working the Steps.*

Getting an SA Sponsor

As we get into the Steps, we find it indispensable to rely for help on those who have gone this way before. In Twelve Step programs, the term commonly used is *sponsor*. What we call the person doesn't matter; and we don't have to call them anything. Asking for help and accepting suggestions are what bring results.

Experienced members advise getting a temporary

sponsor as soon as one is serious about recovery. Later, when we are better established in the fellowship, we can choose another.

Withdrawal from our addiction may leave us in a state of emotional and spiritual shock that can persist for some time. Our sexaholism has so separated us from reality and others that we may appear to others as being "not there." We cannot see the truth about ourselves because we are lost inside ourselves. And for some time, we suffer from tunnel vision, nearsightedness, farsightedness, astigmatism, or all of them put together—anything but normal vision. Some gentle or not-so-gentle holding up of the mirror and prodding are usually necessary, and above all, we need the example of a life that's making it.

We take responsibility for our own recovery, but we don't remain isolated and "in charge" of it. We surrender to God and take direction from the sponsor. Thus, we go to meetings and start making our Connection with people. Alone, we cannot make the transition to reality.

Perfection in the sponsor is neither necessary nor possible. Taking the action of getting out of ourselves is what counts, even though this may not be what we feel like doing. The sponsor can help us conquer the delusion that we should only do what we feel like doing. "Take the action," the sponsor says, "and the feelings will follow. If you wait for the feeling first, it'll never happen."

We discover that in-depth ego-deflation is one of the keys to sobriety and growth, and asking for help often helps us achieve this. Asking for help is one way we start dismantling the wall of ego we've built so carefully around ourselves. In reaching out to another, we reach out to the undiscovered best in ourselves. This confirms our commitment to sobriety and is the beginning of that radical change of attitude from being the center of the universe.

> *"I wanted to stay in charge. That's why God and healing could never get to me."*

There are few absolute requirements a prospective sponsor should have, but a period of comfortable sexual sobriety, including progressive victory over lust, is surely a must. Another requirement is that he or she be ahead of us in working the Steps. The norm is that men sponsor men and women sponsor women. We follow direction and make regular contact, meeting face-to-face when possible once a week or more, especially in the beginning. Some newcomers also find daily phone contact very helpful. The one who needs help does the calling; we give up the old idea of being catered to. Having sponsors with our particular form of acting out doesn't seem to matter as much as having those who are incorporating the principles of the Steps and Traditions in their lives and who "walk like they talk."

Wise sponsors know they can't carry the sexaholic; they can only carry the message of their own recovery. Thus, they do not get involved in giving advice and bearing responsibility *for* the other person. Likewise, we do not become dependent on the sponsor in the way we were with parents, spouses, lovers, or even professionals. The goal of a good sponsor is the eventual *independence* and spiritual and emotional maturity of the individual—to help the person start walking the right path in the right direction. The wise sponsor will also let the person know that their relationship alone is not enough. The person is going to have to make his or her connection with the group and become *part of*.

Typically, when we come into the program, all kinds of personal problems are uppermost in our mind: pending separation or divorce; problems of romance; and occupational, health, legal, or money crises. Most of us felt that if only the problems would go away, we would be okay. What we did not realize was that it is because of and within these very problems that the program works! The program doesn't work in a vacuum; it only works in the day-to-day ebb and flow of our lives. Trial, tribulation, and pain are the soil in which the Steps can germinate, take root, and find fruition in our lives.

Thus, every problem, no matter how small or great; every crisis, resentment, pain, illness, stress, conflict, depression—any and all of them, without exception—can be turned into good. Every time we feel overwhelmed, our sponsor can point the way out of self-pity, resentment, or fear and onto right thinking, helping us say, *"I thank God for the good and the seemingly bad as necessary for my growth. Thy will, not mine, be done."*

The value the sponsors receive, if they are where they should be, is the experience of working their own program in a way otherwise impossible. There is something that only working with others can give us. It is truly a gift, even if the one seeking help is ungrateful or doesn't stay sober. We help, expecting nothing in return, and the measure we receive is the measure we've given of ourselves to another.

First Aid

Here's how two people helped each other stay sober when they had no group:

> I found one other member in a Twelve Step program who also wanted sexual sobriety. I was forty-nine and he was twenty-one. He was single and I was married. I was a college graduate and he was a high school drop-out. We had little in common, but we started calling each other almost daily. We would get current with our lust temptations, telling each other what we were going through to break the power that experience or fantasy had over us. Then, we also started getting current with our resentments. Lust and resentment thus began to evaporate as we brought them to the light, much as sunlight dispels a fog. I call it the "daily double"—getting rid of both daily. When temptation was especially intense, we'd pick up the phone and call right away. Sometimes we'd pray together.
>
> Giving up our lust and resentments to one another as they came up turned out to be a very effective form

of surrender. What a marvelous freedom and joy it brought. And in the process, we were breaking out of that deadly isolation we had locked ourselves into. I look back on that time as one of the highlights of my entrance into the program. I was beginning to come to life.

How It Works—The Practical Reality

This title is adapted from Chapter 5 of *Alcoholics Anonymous*, entitled "How It Works." The books *Alcoholics Anonymous* and *Twelve Steps and Twelve Traditions* (the *Twelve and Twelve*) constitute the basic texts of the original Twelve Step program. This section is not intended to be a comprehensive exposition of the Steps. Our aim here is to try to get at the essential purpose of each Step or group of Steps so they can be readily put into action. The SA program is a program of action.

Everything begins with sobriety. Without sobriety, there is no program of recovery. But without reversing the deadly traits that underlie our addiction, there is no positive and lasting sobriety. To recover from a life based on wrong attitudes, self-obsession, separation, false connections, blindness, and spiritual death requires a program of action that includes a fundamental change in attitude, character change, union, the true Connection, self-awareness, and spiritual life. Working the principles of the Steps as a new way of living has made this happen for us.

No matter how well they are explained, understood, or believed, however, the Steps mean nothing unless they are actually worked out in our thinking and living. *The Steps don't work unless we work them.*

We will try to present a realistic picture of our own experiences in recovery. We trust this will shed light on the path ahead for others and communicate in a direct and personal way how the program works for us. If it seems our feet are too much on the earth, that is because not one of us has ever worked the Steps perfectly. The road was up and down, smooth and rocky. Sometimes we were surrounded by beautiful vistas, at others, we were in a fog and saw nothing but the placing of one foot in front of the other as we trudged ahead. At times we experienced great joy; at other times, doubt, uncertainty, depression, and fear. At times it seemed we were running with winged feet, at others, standing still, and still others, that we were losing ground. But we found that once on this road, something deep within told us it was the right path for us. We simply knew it. And that was enough to keep us going. Whatever our experience, we found it to be the greatest adventure of our lives.

Surrender—Steps One, Two, and Three

Our habit brought us into SA, but it was working Steps One, Two, and Three that brought us into the *program.* There's a difference.

Until we actually experienced these first three Steps, we would never enter the liberating reality of the Twelve. These three were the archway through which we left the old life behind and entered the new life of sobriety and inner peace. They deal with deflation and surrender. The way up is down.

Our way of life brought us to the admission of powerlessness (Step One). Without that we could not see our great need. But the feeling of powerlessness without surrender left us with no real hope. As we saw that others had made this great transition, had been sustained and were now on the freedom road, we gained belief that restoration and new life were possible for us too—"We came to believe" (Step Two). But even this fell short until we completed this threefold attitude change by giving up to God (Step Three). Our habit cut us down; seeing sobriety and the life of God in others gave us the hope; but our own surrender to God brought the Connection that finally worked and kept on working.

At first, the group or sponsor often became the "higher power," since we had left the true God far behind. But if we stayed in that interim condition, it was dangerous, like a car stuck on high-center spinning its wheels and going nowhere. Our own experience taught us that the sooner our surrender was to God—however we understood or did not understand Him—the sooner we made the transition from self to life.

> *"I couldn't just surrender my lust; I had to surrender me."*

A Change of Heart

Steps One, Two, and Three describe the change of heart from self to God, without which no real change in our lives can come about.

There seems to be no such thing as surrender in the abstract. Surrender is a giving up of something specific. Of course, we all had to give up the right to think and practice our habits. What we didn't realize was that we come to this crossroads burdened with a load of other negative attitudes. We found that if we tried surrendering our lust while holding on to our resentment, anger, pride, or dependency, for example, it didn't work. These other passions were often manifested in our attitudes toward parents, authority figures, spouses, or other SA members. For example, one woman discovered that surrender included giving up her right to be nasty to her husband. And one man had to give up emotionally brutalizing his wife and children. Another who wanted to give up street sex but still have a "relationship" discovered he was counting on the relationship to save him from his promiscuity and that surrendering lust has to be all or nothing. And when it came to the marriage bed, many of us discovered it was the last refuge of lust and that here too surrender was the only way. When we finally came to the moment of truth, whatever it was or however slowly we came to it, surrender had to be unconditional.

Surrender as an attitude becomes the key to this spiritual program and the summary of its very essence. Once this initial turnaround is made, it gives us faith in the surrender process. At each subsequent stage there will be a sticking point where a specific attitude or action will have to be acknowledged and dropped before we can be comfortable again. Surrender is not only the key to the Twelve Step program and sexual sobriety, but to a joyous and purposeful life with others.

The surrender required in Steps One, Two, and Three became the fountainhead out of which all things flowed in practicing the other Steps. Because of this attitude change, we would later be able to look at ourselves honestly for what we were and confess it to another (Four and Five). We would be able to acknowledge and unclench our other defects as they became apparent (Six and Seven). Without such a surrender we would never think of taking Steps Eight, Nine, and Ten to begin righting the wrongs to others. And without it we would be unable to have any conscious union with God in prayer and meditation (Eleven) and give ourselves to others (Twelve). Beginning at the beginning was the only way into spiritual recovery for us. *And if we came from some other Twelve Step program, many of us had to begin all over again as though we had never heard of the Steps.* There don't seem to be any short cuts for us.

In summary, for us surrender is the change in attitude of the inner person that makes life possible. It is the great beginning, the insignia and watchword of our program. And no amount of knowledge about surrender can make it a fact until we simply give up, let go, and let God. When we surrender our "freedom," we become truly free.

Step One

"We admitted that we were powerless over lust—
that our lives had become unmanageable."

"I GIVE UP!" It may have come with a loud cry or in a moment of quiet resignation, but the time came when we knew the jig was up. We had been arrested—stopped in our tracks—but we had done it to ourselves. If surrender came only from without, it never "took." When we surrendered out of our own enlightened self-interest, it became the magic key that opened the prison door and set us free.

Arrest and surrender in order to be set free—what a paradox! But it was our self-proclaimed freedom that had been killing us, and we began to see that without limits we would destroy ourselves. But we were powerless to limit ourselves, and the more we indulged, the more unmanageable our lives became. Each lustful act or fantasy became another powerful ray penetrating the nucleus of our psyches and loosening the forces that held us together. Thus, in time we came to the growing realization that we were losing control. It was to this truth that we surrendered—the truth about ourselves.

"Something's WRONG with me, and I can't
fix it!"

Awareness of the unmanageability of our lives was not apparent to us at first. But as we recovered from shock and spiritual blindness, we began to see how we were unable to function without lust, negative attitudes, and dependencies holding our lives together. Reaching the point of utter despair did not always come right away; it came to some of us only after we had been in the fellowship for awhile. The full effect of Step One seems to come gradually or in stages, with the unfolding realization of our unsoundness. It is out of this inner honesty with ourselves that the feelings of hope and forgiveness flow.

We were free to see and admit what we really were inside because we were finally free from having to act out what we were.

How long and how cleverly we had defended our right to wrong ourselves and others, and how long we denied there was any wrong at all! But every wrong attitude and act stored up its own punishment against us from within, until finally, the cumulative weight of our wrongs brought us to our knees.

The Third Option

Before finally giving up, we had tried one or the other of two options: On the one hand, we expressed our obsession by acting it out. On the other hand, we tried suppressing it by drinking, drugging, eating, or by fighting it with white-knuckle willpower. And with what a show of promises and resolutions! Many of us switched from acting out to suppression, back and forth.

Neither option brought us the peace we sought so desperately. Expressing the obsession made it progress relentlessly, on and on, and suppressing it only made the pressure build inside until something had to give. Both options made it worse; we were between a rock and a hard place. We never knew there was another option—surrender. What a beautiful liberating word it has become to those of us who do it!

Surrender is letting go. The story is related in Twelve Step program circles of how monkeys were caught in the wild (it is actually a native folk tale). Fruit as bait is placed in a cage with an opening only large enough to allow the monkey's open hand to enter. Once the monkey's hand grasps the fruit, his fist becomes too large, and his hand is trapped inside. Rather than letting go of the fruit so he can withdraw his hand and go free, the monkey clenches his fist all the harder as he tries to have the fruit and freedom too. Our story!

There is another story of the man who fell off a cliff in the dark and on the way down grasped a branch and hung on for dear life. Weakening, he finally cried out to heaven, "Please help me!" and the answer came, "Let go!" "But if I let go I'll die," the man replied. "Let go!" was all he heard. When finally he could hold on no longer, he did let go, knowing it was the horrible end. To his great surprise, the ground was only a foot below him.

As long as we either clung to it or tried to fight it into submission, our habit fought back, and being more powerful than we, it always won! Only when we let go does the release come, as though God mercifully raises the very earth itself to meet us.

Merely knowing and admitting we were powerless over lust, or whatever form our acting out took, didn't help until we gave up our right to do it and let it go. There was no mistaking this change of heart when it happened; we knew it and those about us knew it. There is no faking surrender. And thank God, when we did give up and stop fighting, He was always there, waiting with open arms. Instead of killing us as we had feared, surrender killed the compulsion!

"I Am a Sexaholic"

Experience has shown us that the public aspect of surrender is crucial. It seems surrender is never complete until it is brought out into the open, into the company of others. This is the great test that separates wishers and whiners from doers.

> *"It's as though I was not really willing to put it down until I brought it out before others who were*

putting theirs down. Making others a part of my surrender helped me be honest with it."

What is this public aspect of surrender? First, it is being able to acknowledge what we are. It takes some of us weeks or months of coming to meetings before we can realize it at depth and say from the inside, "I *am* a sexaholic." Others seem to freely acknowledge this immediately.

Next, we start talking honestly about ourselves; first, what we've done and thought in the lust, sex, and relationship area. Then, gradually, as more is revealed, we talk about our other defects. Typically, these are revealed progressively over time. It's as though we can't see the full extent of the power our sexaholism has over us without first making a start at sharing it in the fellowship. Then we begin to see and disclose more as we become part of the progressive honesty and self-disclosure of others.

A trust begins to develop as we see that nothing is being held against us and that others are just like we are—or worse off. Trust deepens as we become mutually vulnerable by leading with our weaknesses. Leading with our weaknesses becomes the point of identification and union with each other. And it seems someone's self-disclosure has to start it off. Someone takes the risk because he or she has to, the pain is so bad. This helps us pull away the curtain concealing the truth of our own lives and encourages our own self-disclosure. The honesty of one encourages the honesty of others, as though we'd all been waiting for just such a fellowship where we could be on the outside what we really were on the inside all along.

All this takes time. We didn't get here in a day. But before we know it, there is shared honesty and mutual vulnerability. *This is the breakthrough entrance into the Program that will open the way into the healing power of the Steps.* And this is why there must be those in our meetings who are hurting or who have hurt badly enough to break through into true honesty and surrender. This lends power to the meeting, and the spiritual unity and effectiveness of the group are enhanced.

With an in-depth realization of what we really are and

a willingness to reveal the truth about ourselves to other members, we *can* connect with recovery. When we begin telling it like it really is, and was, from the inside out, we become *part of*. The spiritual Connection begins here—by first *disconnecting* from what we did. And we disconnect from it by sending it away from us as we tell it. This is the point of breakthrough.

The essence of effective sharing is that we want to be done with our sexual and other wrongs *and are sending them away*. Mere catharsis or even honest self-disclosure misses the mark if that's all it is. The aim is to bring our diseased attitudes and misdeeds to the light of others and God to *be done with them*. When it comes from such an attitude, sharing becomes a liberating and life-giving experience.

This is why "telling all" is not taking the First Step. Such confession can be anything from boastful replay to anguished dumping or intellectual analysis. And even then, it's not really "all" and often is only surface material. In truth, we don't "take" the First Step; it takes us. It overtakes us. And if it hasn't yet, hopefully it will. The sickness and punishment sexaholism produces inside us keep pounding us until we're ready to give up, let go, and know we are powerless over lust.

". . . Our Lives Had Become Unmanageable"

For those who enter recovery through this program, the realization of powerlessness becomes coupled with growing awareness of personal unmanageability—the fact that something is out of kilter at the core of the self. For it is our very self that has turned from life. If we are content with ourselves, simply minus the compulsion, there can be no *recovery*. Recovery is more than mere sobriety.

Deep inside we always knew there were other things wrong with us, and it turns out our addictions were really trying to keep us from facing them. This is why, once the initial surrender of Steps One, Two, and Three is made,

Steps Four through Ten deal with exposing, confessing, and righting our wrongs.

In sobriety we quickly learn that we are just as powerless over other defects that begin to surface (resentment, for example) as we ever were over lust, sex, and dependency. The fact that these other problems aren't necessarily as obvious as lust can seduce us into the notion we're really okay. We can go for stretches of time without acting out on them, but when things go wrong, watch out! They burst forth with a fearsome vengeance and fury. Bad feelings boil up as if out of nowhere—feelings that are against others, that isolate us and force us back into the prison-house of the self. We'd rather believe such outbursts are simply results of what others are doing to us, unwilling to see that we think and act badly because there's something wrong inside *us*. As though bitter waters can spring up from a pure well.

What great relief to finally come to the place where we can say, not only "I'm powerless over lust," but "I'm powerless over *me*!"

It's okay to be absolutely powerless over self. This is where we join the human race. And best of all, just as the admission of powerlessness over lust is the key to our sexual sobriety, so the admission of powerlessness over our defects is the key to our emotional sobriety. *Victory through powerlessness by the grace of God.* What a glorious liberating discovery!

This is the point at which our self-honesty begins to grow, where recovery begins. But thank God, our defects are revealed to us progressively. In the fellowship of identification, acceptance, and forgiveness we are able to bear the realization without destroying ourselves or resorting to one of our drugs to escape. Our God is patient and loving and kind with us; as we must learn to be with others.

The program calls those who are tired and weighed down with the burden of self, those who want to be rid of the load but can't. It calls those who are trapped in the prison of self but know no way out. A broken and contrite spirit—the spirit of the First Step—is the key that opens the door and sets us free.

Step Two

"Came to believe that a power greater than ourselves could restore us to sanity."

Not God

We can almost hear a newcomer say, "I thought this was a self-help program! What do you mean, I can't stay sober, joyous, and free without God!" Or, as the *Twelve and Twelve* says,

> Look what you people have done to us! . . . Having reduced us to a state of absolute helplessness, you now declare that none but a Higher Power can remove our obsession. Some of us *won't* believe in God, others can't, and still others who do believe that God exists have no faith whatever He will perform this miracle. Yes, you've got us over the barrel, all right—but where do we go from here? (p. 25)

The first three words of Step Two give us the key to this dilemma:

We *came*
We *came to*
We *came to believe.*

We began by simply coming to meetings. Then, somewhere along the line, we "came to"—we awoke to the reality of our situation, came out of emotional and spiritual shock, and came to the reality of a power at work in the lives of others who were sober. Then, we came to believe. For many of us this translated into the startling—though welcome—conclusion that we were *not God.*

When we cast ourselves on the mercy of the group, we are, in effect, resorting to a power greater than ourselves. After all, we admit, many of these people are staying sexually sober, and some had it worse than we. More than this, we feel a strength and presence in fellowship. The spirit of the meeting often seems to be greater than the sum of its members. This gives us hope and draws us into the light. Soon, we find ourselves making our own personal Connection. Here's how one person put it:

> *"At first, all I believed in was my sickness and lack of faith. Soon, however, I was telling myself, 'I hope it's all true.' Then, I began acting as if it were, and faith in the program itself was established. As I became more honest and open to the truth in others, I came to believe that others had faith. Finally, genuine faith in a higher Power came ever so slowly as a God of my very own and a faith that worked for* me."

Surrendering to the Truth about Ourselves

The second half of Step Two, ". . .could restore us to sanity," was not hard for many of us to acknowledge; our First Step had revealed at least some of our irrational thinking and behavior. And we slowly began to realize that such loss of control *was* a form of insanity. But just as an unsound mind was the inevitable by-product of our attitudes and wrongs, its healing would be the by-product of working the Steps. There is great promise here. *Restoration to sanity* becomes a very real hope, because we see it happening around us. Sanity is contagious!

Sometimes the program comes harder to those who are "believers" than to those who never had any faith at all or who had lost it. This often holds true for those who have been in other Twelve Step programs before coming to SA. One might think that previous religious devotion or success in quitting another addiction would make it easier for one to gain sexual sobriety, but this is not necessarily the case. Often, such members find they must start "from square one," as though they had no faith or had never heard of the program. A chain is only as strong as its weakest link, the saying goes, and lack of surrender in any of our known defective areas blocks the grace of God and makes it impossible to forge any chain of enduring spiritual and emotional strength. Success in quitting other addictions seduced many of us into believing we were really working the program and had everything together. The unmanageability of our lives proved otherwise. Many of us merely switched addictions.

Knowledge and pride were our chief obstacles here. Knowing the Truth, or knowing the Program—often being self-styled authorities and even sponsoring others—only kept us from changing our attitudes and righting our wrongs. *Knowledge never gave us power.* We had left lust, sex, and relationships out of the exposure, surrender, and recovery process, which simply meant we could not fully recover. No wonder we were still uncomfortable! "Half measures availed us nothing." It seems harder for some who have been sober for years from other addictions to admit they are in denial in the sexaholic area than it is for newcomers who have never even heard of the Steps. This is simply one of the realities of our experience.

We discovered the hard way that we had to leave our knowledge and pride outside the door when we entered. We could only join with our fellow members and be a *part of* when we identified on the basis of our *current* addiction, powerlessness, and distress. We identify with each other at the point of our weaknesses. Our wrongfulness and our wrongs are what bring us together and to God.

Many of us have already been through the alcohol, drug, pill, and overeating scenes. We've become aware of our compulsive approach to almost everything in our lives. There's no place left to go except to face the truth about ourselves, stop resorting to other addictions and forms of lust we think we can get away with, and surrender to our God.

Step Three

"Made a decision to turn our will and our lives over to the care of God as we understood Him."

The Turning Point

The first recovering alcoholics, out of whose experiences the Twelve Step program was forged, had a tough saying: "Find God or die!" Alcohol has a way of destroying the body. In a different sense, this is also our dilemma: "Find your true Connection or lose your self!" Lust has a way of destroying the soul. In Step Three we surrender our defiance and become reconciled to our God.

We discovered that the root of our problem is conscious separation from the Source of our lives; the solution is conscious union with that Source. Thus, coming to the end of ourselves in surrender brought us to the place where we could finally let God have a personal place in our lives.

> Practicing Step Three is like the opening of a door which to all appearances is still closed and locked. All we need is a key, and the decision to swing the door open. There is only one key, and it is called willingness. Once unlocked by willingness, the door opens almost of itself, and looking through it, we shall see a

> pathway beside which is an inscription. It reads: "This is the way to a faith that works." In the first two steps we were engaged in reflection. We saw that we were powerless . . . but we also perceived that faith of some kind . . . is possible to anyone. These conclusions did not require action; they required only acceptance.
>
> Like all remaining steps, Step Three calls for affirmative action, for it is only by action that we can cut away the self-will which has always blocked the entry of God . . . into our lives. . . . Therefore our problem now becomes just how and by what specific means shall we be able to let Him in? Step Three represents our first attempt to do this. In fact, the effectiveness of the whole . . . program will rest upon how well and earnestly we have tried to come to a "decision to turn our will and our lives over to the care of God *as we understood Him.*" (*Twelve and Twelve*, pp. 34–35)

The AA text goes on to examine the role of dependence in our lives and our ruinous self-sufficiency and concludes:

> So it is by circumstance rather than by any virtue that we have been driven to AA, have admitted defeat, have acquired the rudiments of faith, and now want to make a decision to turn our will and our lives over to a Higher Power. (*Twelve and Twelve*, p. 38)

> It is when we try to make our will conform with God's that we begin to use it rightly. To all of us, this was a most wonderful revelation. *Our whole trouble had been the misuse of willpower. We had tried to bombard our problems with it instead of attempting to bring it into agreement with God's intention for us.* To make this increasingly possible is the purpose of AA's Twelve Steps, and Step Three opens the door. (p. 40)

Taking Step Three is a matter of the heart, but as with most of the other Steps, bringing our intentions into the light of another person or group has a power that the best of intentions on one's own do not. The road to our hell was paved with good intentions and fine resolve. Taking Step Three is best done with our sponsor or an understanding person on the program. We are cautioned, however, that it is better to meet God alone than with one who might misunderstand. The words we use, of course, are quite optional so long as we express the true desire of our hearts, voicing it without reservation, making sure we can at last abandon ourselves utterly to Him. Here is the Third Step prayer:

> "God, I offer myself to Thee—to build with me and to do with me as Thou wilt. Relieve me of the bondage of self, that I may better do Thy will. Take away my difficulties, that victory over them may bear witness to those I would help of Thy Power, Thy Love, and Thy Way of life. May I do Thy will always!" (*Alcoholics Anonymous*, p. 63)

One Day at a Time

Once we've taken Step Three, it is easier to begin to practice it in our daily lives. In times of emotional disturbance or indecision, we can pause, ask for quiet, and in the stillness simply say:

> "God grant me the serenity to accept the things I cannot change, courage to change the things I can, and wisdom to know the difference. Thy will, not mine, be done." (*Twelve and Twelve*, p. 41)

We become able to transcend lust more and more by calling on God's power to expel the obsession, surrender temptation, and trust Him in all things. As we do this, we learn to begin each day with the same type of commitment, asking God to keep us sober for just that day, "One Day at a Time." This means we are learning to live without lust and really *want* to be free. One member's prayer is

> *"Lord, I surrender my lust and ask you to keep me sober from my lust today because I cannot; but by your strength, I can."*

Many of us also, before going to sleep, surrender our lust again and ask to be kept free of it throughout the night. We discovered we had to surrender the entire self—subconscious included—for lust had permeated our entire being.

In simple but profound words, the whole program can be reduced to what someone discovered for himself:

"Without God, I can't;
Without me, God won't."

May you turn to Him now.

Making the Wrongs Right—Steps Four Through Ten

The Toughest Act in Town

Sadly, many men and women with years of physical sobriety on Twelve Step programs never make the breakthrough into the heart of the program and true recovery. The biggest obstacle seems to be Steps Four through Ten—the core substance of the program. It is these Steps that seem to be the least realized in actual experience. When first exposed to these Steps, many of us balk. The process of righting wrongs is foreign to us. It seems light years away, in another dimension; we can't connect with it. We either dismiss it out of hand or say to ourselves, "I'm doing fine just like I am." Blindness and denial. It is as though we will go to any lengths to avoid doing what is required for our own healing. When some members see that such persons are captive to externals rather than having an awakening to life, they have been overheard to say, "If sobriety is all there is, I want no part of it!" There are few things so pitiful as an aborted spiritual life. The amazing thing is that we can give the *appearance* of life, even though we are dead.

There is one sure way to get more than mere physical sobriety, and that is by coming out of denial, seeing our wrongs, and righting them under God—making Steps Four through Ten a way of life. The result is *a new life.* And with us sexaholics, it is doubtful that we can even maintain sexual sobriety without this, although many of us try. The more we are willing to listen to the experience and success of others, the more faith we get in this process. We ask for willingness to try this path, even though we may feel sure it is not for us. Once we do try it, we're sold.

Encounter

Perhaps this is the place to tell a true story from a member who says he always learns things the hard way (some details are changed to protect the other party).

> The people in our little community have to rely on a woman who runs the neighborhood hardware store to get their local mail. Everyone complains about her sour disposition and intimidation. Knowing how I want to break out into resentment every time I see her, I usually give up the right to do so before walking in, and hold my peace.
>
> But the other day, she baited me again, and instead of saying nothing, I challenged her, with some heat behind my words. And of course, she promptly read me off. Before she had gotten the last word out, I got loud, told her that was the last time I wanted to hear from her big mouth, and stomped out.
>
> I hadn't really lost control, I thought, and knew I was fully justified, feeling pretty smug about the whole thing, until three days later, when the incident kept playing back in my mind. Each time it came up, I'd replay the scene as though I were in court, pleading my case before a judge, winning every time! But it persisted, until I was willing to ask for willingness to look at it honestly.

I concluded that my disturbance indicated something was wrong with *me*; that over and above whatever she had said, *I* had done something wrong. I had retaliated, trying to hit back. I could have challenged her without doing so. I had found a pretext to reject her and push her away—that old pattern that has plagued me all my life. So only I knew that *I* was wrong and that the cause of my disturbance was me.

I had been binging on food and television ever since it happened for no apparent reason. I couldn't even pray without the scene coming back. What I discovered was that I could not get rid of that memory, and that if I didn't make it right, I'd have to keep on covering it, coating it over, or drowning it out with something.

I asked for courage, surrendered my fear and pride, went back to the store, and told the woman I had been wrong in yelling at her. Unexpectedly, she looked at me with pained eyes and tried to explain. Instead of becoming angry, defensive, or abusive, as I had feared, she was broken and vulnerable, and I was moved to compassion. Since I can seldom express this emotion because I'm a love cripple, I knew that for my sake, I had to "take the action," despite my natural inhibition. Thank God I had been taught to do what did *not* come naturally by those who had gone before me in the program. I put my hand on her arm, and that connection drew me to her; it broke the impasse of fear, anger, and pride within me. I even wanted to embrace her.

Tears welled in her eyes as she glanced at me shamefully, hung her head, then looked up again, as though she was just as surprised as I at the gift of life flowing between us. In that timeless moment where we looked at each other, each knowing he or she had been wrong, each forgiving the other, there was spiritual union—a most marvelous and transcendent experience, a fullness of glory and great joy. I left the store feeling transformed, full of light and a great liberating energy.

Natural Law

Now let's look at what was happening in this encounter and try to derive the spiritual laws at work here in our common experience:

1. We do something wrong; the reason we do it doesn't matter; the wrong in the other person doesn't matter.
2. There is an immediate and inevitable effect within us. It disturbs our equilibrium. It throws us out of kilter.
3. We don't like to feel disturbed; it's uncomfortable; so we instinctively try to quiet the disturbance.
4. Our first try is denial; we try to justify and rationalize to ourselves.
5. When that doesn't provide relief, we're left with only two other choices, either to treat the distress or treat the *cause* of the distress.
6. The only way we can treat the cause of our distress and right the wrong is to make amends to the person we wronged.
7. As soon as we acknowledge our wrong, we start feeling better, and when we make the amends, we're set free. The tyranny of the memory and the guilt are gone. We *feel* free, released. And if the other person is forgiving, he himself is freed, and there is spiritual union with that person, as in the above story.

In relating this experience in a meeting, the member remarked afterwards,

> *"This formula fixes me faster than anything! Instant success! The words, 'I was wrong,' which I was forever trying to extort from others, become, when I make them mine, the most wonderful words in the world. They bring peace to me! How can something that felt so bad turn into such great good?"*

Notice that the same negative spiritual process at work in the addiction (Part I) comes back into play every time we do something wrong. We can't get around it: For every wrong action, there's a negative reaction within *us.*

> *"I'm not only my own worst enemy, I'm the only real enemy I've got! What I* do *is what I get."*

Technically speaking, the man in the above story was making a Tenth Step (if tardy) amends. The point of telling this story here is that looking at ourselves and making amends embodies the principle underlying all of Steps Four through Ten. The entire heart of the program has us working on ourselves. The key to recovery and spiritual growth is the righting of our wrongs. It dissolves our guilt, sets us free, and energizes us with joy and strength.

Righting our wrongs thus becomes the single most powerful tool for success in spiritual growth and recovery. Why? (1) It gets the wrong out of the way so God can work in us. (2) Taking such repeated actions begins to loosen the hold over us of one defect at a time.

No wonder this is the exercise we dread the most; it's strong medicine. And most of us prefer some easier, softer way. So we might as well put our hearts to it and begin working these Steps in earnest; there is no way around them if we want to recover.

We might ask, "How is it that righting wrongs becomes freeing and healing? What's really happening in this process?" At best, all we can offer as answer are analogies, since our inner reality doesn't lend itself to precise description.

Let's think back on the scene in the hardware store. Doing wrong to the woman produced a self-destructive effect in the man. Making the wrong right not only counteracted that negative effect but created an impulse of positive energy that was healing and creative. *Thus, if for every wrong there's a negative reaction within us that takes away life, for every act of doing right, there's a positive reaction that produces life.*

This law of our spiritual biology plays such an important part in our recovery that we might break it out as a separate step: *"Took the actions of love to improve our rela-*

tions with others." But this fruition cannot begin until we have made that great turnaround in Steps Four through Ten. More about this later.

Recovery

Another reason why righting our wrongs must be part of our recovery is that this is how we reverse the deadly separation at work in the addictive process and restore union. To the extent we surrender and stop practicing our defects, righting the wrongs they cause, we experience union within ourselves—wholeness—union with others, and with God.

Only true union fills the void our sick connections were trying to satisfy. But finding God, or finding spiritual union with another is not the result of a search at all, but of a moral housecleaning. As an AA oldtimer has said, when we *uncover* and *discard* our wrong attitudes and actions, we *discover* our true selves, others, and God. God is not something added in from the outside. He is someone we discover on the inside when we clear away the wreckage.

Uncovering ourselves is what makes union possible. How can we be whole if part of us is hiding from ourselves?

Thus, the grand equation for getting well and filling the great void at the heart of our lives is

Uncover ——→ Discard ——→ Discover

Steps One, Two, and Three bring us to the point where we are able to start this process, and once begun, the healing work of Steps Four through Ten becomes a way of life. Each cycle of awareness, surrender, and discovery produces growth, union, and sight, which bring about more awareness, surrender, and discovery. The road narrows as we go, but since there is always more revealed within us to discard, our sight improves, and the vista becomes incredibly more wonderful and fulfilling. Many of us identify with the excitement of one member's discovery:

> *"Righting my wrongs is where the Connection is! So every time I surrender my desire to lust or*

> *resent and take God's deliverance, I've experienced union with God! Can you believe that? I can't, but it's true. And every time I surrender my desire to judge or condemn another or hang on to self-centered fear—every time I'm doing what I have to do to stay comfortable—I'm getting united. What a gift!*
>
> *And whenever I fail and* do *the wrong, uncovering it to another and making amends not only make it right but produce union too. This has to be the most unbelievable thing in the universe."*

Having now come to the end of self and surrendered in the first three Steps, we are ready to begin taking the stairs upward toward recovery, healing, and growth from Step Four onward. These actions bring us face to face with the dreaded monster we've been running from—ourselves. They encourage and enable us to see the uglies within so we can become willing to change. Every liability will turn out to be an avenue of grace. And like a magic looking glass, they first help us see ourselves, and then, as we gain courage, help us jump through and enter that new kingdom we could never know before.

Now is when we start unloading that burden of wrongs and guilt we had been heaping on our backs. From out of great despair comes true surrender, which releases within us the desire to be good and make things right with our fellow man. If we cannot bring ourselves to do this, we have surely not yet passed through the gate of Step Three. Better to stop and go no further lest in pretending to work the other Steps, we seal over our wrongs like an infected cyst. No one seems able to make the Third Step commitment while knowingly holding on to his or her wrongs.

But just as surely as our wrongs are what brought us to despair, so our surrender to God and others in our wrongs will open the doorway to that great release and transformation that await us. Healing takes place from the inside out, and we come to see the truth in the ancient proverb,

"He who conceals his transgressions will not prosper, but he who confesses and forsakes them will obtain mercy."

We are the doctor in this soul-surgery, and we perform the operation without any painkillers. Thank God we're not alone; those who have gone before us have put themselves under the knife and have come out into the bright sunlight of a new life, emerging to know themselves, others, and God, and the very beauty of life itself. This is our finest odyssey.

Step Four

"Made a searching and fearless moral inventory of ourselves."

Facing the Wild Elephant

Something inside us always knew we'd have to face ourselves, but we kept running away, refusing to take that long deep look into the mirror. And the longer we put it off, the more we resorted to our drug to cover the feelings and guilt, which produced an even uglier image we had to flee the more.

We were like the man in the ancient parable who, fleeing a wild elephant, takes refuge in a well. He hangs on to two branches over the opening, while his feet rest on objects jutting out from the sides. Suspended from one branch is a hive of honey, which he starts eating. The pleasure this gives him, plus the darkness of the well, keep him from seeing that two rats, one black and the other white, are gnawing away at the branches from which he hangs; that what he's standing on are really four snakes, thrusting their heads out of their holes; and that below him is a dragon with gaping jaws waiting to devour him.

The two rats, we are told, are night and day, which successively eat away at the span of our lives. The four snakes represent those basic elements in our system that keep us in equilibrium. The honey is the pleasure of the senses, whose deceptive sweetness seduces us to ruin. And the dragon is the inevitable end that awaits us all. The wild elephant, we might add, is the self we're running from, fear of which drives us on our mad flight into that dark hole where we prefer to stay and hide.

When we come out of hiding, turn, and face this terrible beast in our Fourth and Fifth Steps, he disappears. In his place stands that exposed and erring self we had left behind—the real we.

Without facing the truth about ourselves, there is no hope for lasting sobriety, serenity, and freedom.

> *"I could never figure out why knowing the truth about God never set me free. Or the truth about psychology or the Twelve Step program. But when I finally came to the place where I saw the truth about* me*—and despaired. . . . Well,* that *was the beginning."*

What a relief to finally face the great FEAR—ourselves! We always knew that's what we had to do, but we hung on to our misery too long, and after a certain point, found we were powerless to let go. So when we determine to go ahead with Step Four, we "pocket our pride and go to it, illuminating every twist of character, every dark cranny of the past." (*Alcoholics Anonymous*, p. 75)

If the admission of powerlessness brought us to our change of attitude and reconciled us to God (Steps One, Two, and Three), the truth about ourselves became the raw material from which our new lives would be built. Only the self as it really is can be changed and live and grow; the one hiding in the well will surely die.

> By now the newcomer has probably arrived at the following conclusions: that his character defects, representing instincts gone astray, have been the primary cause of his drinking and his

failure at life; that unless he is now willing to work hard at the elimination of the worst of these defects, both sobriety and peace of mind will still elude him; that all the faulty foundation of his life will have to be torn out and built anew on bedrock. (*Twelve and Twelve*, p. 50)

The Moral Inventory

What is a Fourth Step inventory? Listen to what *Alcoholics Anonymous* and the *Twelve and Twelve* call it:

A personal housecleaning

A fact-finding and fact-facing process

An effort to discover the truth about ourselves

A search for flaws in our make-up which caused our failures

Since it was self that had defeated us, we consider its common manifestations: resentment, anger, grudges, fear.

We look for our own mistakes—where we were to blame: selfish, dishonest, self-seeking, frightened.

We admit our wrongs honestly and are willing to set these matters straight.

We describe the hurt we have done others.

We discover the choices and attitudes that drove us into acting out the role we have chosen to play.

(From *Alcoholics Anonymous*, chapter 5.)

This perverse soul-sickness is not pleasant to look upon. Instincts on rampage balk at investigation. The minute we make a serious attempt to probe them, we are liable to suffer severe reactions.

If temperamentally we are on the depressive side, we are apt to be swamped with guilt and self-loathing. . . . If, however, our natural disposition is inclined to self-righteousness or grandiosity, our reaction will be just the opposite. We will be offended at . . . suggested inventory. . . . We believe that our one-time good characters will be revived the moment we quit. . . . If we were pretty nice people all along, except for our drinking, what need is there for a moral inventory now that we are sober?

> We also clutch at another wonderful excuse for avoiding an inventory. Our present anxieties and troubles, we cry, are caused by the behavior of other people—people who *really* need a moral inventory. . . . Therefore we think our indignation is justified and reasonable—that our resentments are the "right kind." *We* aren't the guilty ones. *They* are! . . . people who are driven by pride of self unconsciously blind themselves to their liabilities. (*Twelve and Twelve*, pp. 44–46)

Listen to the frank admission of one person who, it turns out, after many sincere tries, could not connect with either sobriety or the program:

> *"I dread the Fourth. I have the feeling that not only will I have to tell it to someone, but that I'll then have to* do *something about it all. And I don't want to do anything like that; I just want to be fixed."*

Locked into such an attitude, we could never break free; and only we can change that attitude. For the above person it could have been the beginning of recovery. There is no dread to the release and joy that our Fourth Step can bring. At this point our experience parallels that of the alcoholics exactly:

> Pride says, "You need not pass this way," and Fear says, "You dare not look!" But the testimony of AA's who have really tried a moral inventory is that pride and fear of this sort turn out to be bogeymen, nothing else. Once we have a complete willingness to take inventory, and exert ourselves to do the job thoroughly, a wonderful light falls upon this foggy scene. As we persist, a brand-new kind of confidence is born, and the sense of relief at finally facing ourselves is indescribable. (*Twelve and Twelve*, pp. 49–50)

How We Go About It

This business of the Fourth Step inventory need cause no confusion. It is, in fact, very simple. Writing our Fourth is writing about ourselves—who we really are. And since our defects didn't come about in a vacuum, we can pretty well reveal the truth about ourselves by telling about our relations and encounters with other people.

One way to go about it is to take up, one at a time, any person or incident we have bad feelings about. Describing the feelings we had at the time and examining them, we then ask ourselves what we did wrong or how our attitude was wrong. The simple procedure and examples given in Chapter 5 of *Alcoholics Anonymous* have proven helpful to many here.

No one has ever taken the perfect or complete Fourth. Many have found great value in doing it again in later stages of growth and awareness. A well-organized or well-written inventory may be no true inventory at all. The Fourth is the *person*, and in the emotional area, people are not computers. Human emotions don't travel in straight lines, they zigzag all over. It is not necessary to slavishly follow someone else's outline, format, or procedure. We write about ourselves as best we can. The key is looking at our own defects and wrongs, especially in our relations with others. Whether we proceed one defect at a time or one person or incident at a time usually becomes clear as we begin. And once we start, we open up the blocked channels, and it all starts coming out.

All our wrong attitudes and actions have to get out, so we *write* them out. We set them down in black and white so we can see ourselves face to face. When it's down in writing, we can't quickly turn away and forget what we saw, as in a mirror's fleeting image.

If we find we are blocked on the past, there's no sense trying to force it. We pray for willingness. If we find we cannot do it without undue erotic arousal, something is wrong; a talk with one's sponsor is indicated. Better to look forward to being able to look at ourselves in a different spirit. In such a case, the aborted attempt has already told us that something about our attitude needs more surrender.

Even though it seems impossible and unnatural for us, we make a searching and fearless inventory of ourselves. We do it *because* we don't want to! And this becomes part of the great adventure of doing the difficult. Knowing there will be another human being we'll share it with, one who has gone through his or her own Fourth and Fifth Steps, we face looking at our darkest secrets and misdeeds and get them all down on paper. Taking responsibility for our own recovery begins in earnest with the Fourth Step inventory.

The Payoff

There's another reason why the inventory is a must. How can we ever experience forgiveness and freedom from our wrongs unless we bring them out? Getting our secrets out into the open is one of the first concrete demonstrations that we want to change and starts an ongoing process that will continue to bear good fruit. The Fourth and Fifth Steps can be the beginning of a lifelong ability to increasingly face ourselves and take responsibility for our own recovery. Recovery and healing await us when we open this door to the miracle of spiritual union with ourselves and others, and, without even realizing it, union with the Source of our lives. Until we can write out our Fourth Step, we apparently cannot see or face ourselves; until we give it away to another, we aren't willing to let go of our wrongs and be free.

Step Five

"Admitted to God, to ourselves, and to another human being the exact nature of our wrongs."

It takes a moment of courage. Whenever we're ready to give up the wrongs revealed in our Fourth Step, we take the leap and give it away to another. Clinging to that which is killing us is clinging to the curse. When we admit the exact nature of our wrongs to another, we are finally admitting the truth to ourselves and to God. Without this principle active in our lives, we have no hope for lasting sobriety, serenity, and freedom.

> *"I took Step Five with my sponsor and experienced freedom from the burden of my past guilt. No big deal, just a quiet realization that I was part of the human race. I belonged."*

Thus, the Fifth Step is another surrender. We give up the right to continue practicing the diseased attitudes and actions revealed therein and give up our sick isolation. Surrendering in this way brings us out into the light. It is the acid test of our ability to be honest about ourselves. If we cannot do this with another, how can we ever hope to have an honest confession or relation with our God?

Bringing the Inside out

The principle of Step Five is also the key to having group SA meetings that come to life. We identify and have true union with others on the basis of our revealed weaknesses. And Step Five gives us as individuals this initial breakthrough, which we can then work out in our daily lives and fellowship with others in meetings.

Listen to what the AA texts have to say about Step Five:

> But they had not learned enough of humility, fearlessness, and honesty, in the sense we find it necessary, until they told someone else *all* their life story. . . . We must be entirely honest with somebody if we expect to live long or happily in this world. (*Alcoholics Anonymous*, pp. 73–74)

> Once we have taken this step, withholding nothing, we are delighted. We can look the world in the eye. We can be alone at perfect peace and ease. Our fears fall from us. We begin to feel the nearness of our Creator. (p. 75)

> If we have come to know how wrong thinking and action have hurt us and others, then the need to quit living by ourselves with those tormenting ghosts of yesterday gets more urgent than ever. We have to talk to somebody about them. (*Twelve and Twelve*, p. 55)

> Relief never came by confessing the sins of other people. Everybody had to confess his own. (p. 56)

> The grace of God will not enter to expel our destructive obsessions until we are willing to try this. (p. 57)

> We shall get rid of that terrible sense of isolation we've always had. (p. 57)

> Until we had talked with complete candor of our conflicts, and had listened to someone else do the same thing, we still didn't belong. Step Five was the answer. It was the beginning of true kinship with man and God. (p. 57)

> Our moral inventory had persuaded us that all-round forgiveness was desirable, but it was only when we resolutely tackled Step Five that we inwardly *knew* we'd be able to receive forgiveness and give it, too. (p. 58)

> Only by discussing ourselves, holding back nothing, only by being willing to take advice and accept direction could we set foot on the road to straight thinking, solid honesty, and genuine humility. (p. 59)
>
> Until we actually sit down and talk aloud about what we have so long hidden, our willingness to clean house is still largely theoretical. When we are honest with another person, it confirms that we have been honest with ourselves and with God. (p. 60)

A Very Special Time

Ideally, the Fifth Step should be taken with one's sponsor, the one who should know us better than anyone and the one we trust the most. In subsequent dealings with us it will work to their advantage, and to ours, if they have the benefit of this in-depth self-disclosure.

Ample time should be allowed; ideally, it should be left open-ended. This is too important an experience to be subject to schedules, interruptions, or distractions. It is a unique, private, and confidential encounter between two human beings, a time of quiet resonance between two open lives. To work it through from beginning to end, with sponsor identification and feedback, can take hours. It should be done in one session so that awareness, continuity, and momentum are not compromised. If the Fourth Step has been prepared well, only minimal interruption from the sponsor will be necessary. He may wish to identify parallels in his own experience to give support and encouragement. He may want to raise questions, but most often, these are left till later.

The one doing his or her Fifth can be told in effect, "This is *your* time, *your* story. I encourage you to reveal yourself completely, leaving no part of your wrong acts or feelings undisclosed." Some may wish to ask for guidance and help in prayer together before starting. The sponsor may want to pray for a listening ear and an understanding heart.

After the person has revealed every uncomfortable feeling and wrong that he or she can recount, there should be a time for assessment. What does the story reveal about this person? Does he have the capacity to be honest and self-revealing? Has he confessed the details of even the most shameful incidents and feelings? Does he see himself correctly? Is he willing to see and admit his wrong attitudes and actions, his destructive relations with others, his self-obsession and dishonesty? Is he willing to change and right his wrongs? Is he willing to be confronted with himself? Is he willing to accept responsibility for his recovery and take direction?

In certain cases, individuals might be asked to review the inventory again, perhaps for another session, and, in every case where they have revealed negative relations with others, to ask themselves, Where was *I* wrong in my attitude, and what does this tell me about *myself*?

We caution the person working through the Fifth about a possible letdown afterward. Putting off the old self with all its wrongs can leave us exposed and vulnerable and with the feeling that there is nothing of substance left. This is where the sponsor comes in, helping turn such negative feelings into forgiveness, hope, healing, and love.

The *Twelve and Twelve* says it best:

> This feeling of being at one with God and man, this emerging from isolation through the open and honest sharing of our terrible burden of guilt, brings us to a resting place where we may prepare ourselves for the following Steps toward a full and meaningful sobriety. (p. 62)

The giving and receiving of the Fifth Step is a precious experience for both parties. Time stands still, and we meet another human being in the deepest inner sanctuary of our souls, often where no one has been before. There is true spiritual union here—communion. And spiritual awakenings are born here, for God is here.

Steps Six and Seven

"Were entirely ready to have God remove all these defects of character."

"Humbly asked Him to remove our shortcomings."

Pain

If we're on the right road, there inevitably comes a time when we cry out to God, "I'm tired of this defect; I want to be free of it! Please take it away!" The recurring distress it causes us, not to mention others, gets progressively more acute until it outweighs whatever pleasure or false support it was providing. This humbling realization, this moment of clarity, usually illumines one defect at a time. It is the essence of Steps Six and Seven.

It is often easy, having just taken Step Five with our sponsor, to "take" Six and Seven, declaring to sponsor, God, and the whole world that we resolve to put away our wrongs. This puts us on record as wanting to go in the right direction. But it's another thing to become free of the power these defects have over us. As with lust and our sexual addiction, we must take responsibility and the necessary actions so the grace of God can give us victory over these other shortcomings too.

Steps One through Five should have the natural and inevitable effect of creating in us a new heart that wants to do right. Note that the wording of Step Six, "Were entirely ready . . ." depicts a state of mind issuing from a prior change of attitude. If this state of mind is not present, something is amiss. The crucial attitude change that should have accompanied Steps One through Five—surrender—has never taken place.

Surrender—Again

We do an initial Steps Six and Seven, usually following the taking of our Fifth Step, when our awareness and resolve to be rid of our shortcomings are high. Without this willingness and initial surrender, we're not going anywhere in this new adventure in reality. We come to the place where we are entirely ready to start this healing process by surrendering the right to hang on to our defects (Six); then we ask to have them removed (Seven). (We understand from AA that the two words *defects* and *shortcomings* refer to the same thing.)

One way to start this process is to make a list of all the defects of character that were revealed in our Fourth and Fifth Steps. Then, when ready to let them go, we ask God to give us the power to overcome them. The Seventh Step prayer in Chapter 6 of *Alcoholics Anonymous* can be helpful as a starter:

> "My Creator, I am now willing that you should have all of me, good and bad. I pray that you now remove from me every single defect of character which stands in the way of my usefulness to you and my fellows. Grant me strength, as I go out from here, to do your bidding. Amen." (p. 76)

Action

We ask God to remove our defects, but *we* start taking the actions required, for "Faith without action is dead." On a daily, hourly, moment-by-moment basis we begin. Usually, it's one defect at a time, every time it shows up. One incident, one encounter, one trial at a time, we stop, look, and listen to our feelings and review what happened. Sometimes we have to write it out to see it. No matter what wrong the other party has done, *if we are disturbed, there is always something wrong with us.* Especially in the area of attitude.

If we don't see what's wrong, we ask for the willingness to do so. When we see it, we acknowledge it and ask for courage and wisdom to make it right. Then we go make it right, leaving the results up to God. The results inside *us* are immediate; we are overcoming our defect.

> *"This is without a doubt the greatest therapeutic process known to man. It works every single time! I'm not subject to Fate anymore; I have a choice! I can change the course of my life! I can change me!"*

In Steps Six and Seven we surrender the defects uncovered in our inventory. In Steps Eight, Nine, and Ten we amend our past and present wrongs. In actual practice, these Steps all work together. We can't surrender our defects without making right the wrongs they cause. And conversely, making right the wrongs they've caused helps us surrender our defects.

> *"That must be why none of the help I sought ever changed me; I had to change myself. And for some reason, I can't fix myself without fixing what I do to others."*

No matter how much we come to know about the Twelve Step program, it is the actions we take to let go of our defects that bring the results. And dramatic results they are.

An Ongoing Process

In recovery we find that Steps Six and Seven, once taken, become a continuing process. And rather than being a matter of eradication of the impulses to think or do wrong, it is freedom from their power over us, one temptation at a time. The defect itself may remain, but we no longer have to obey it. When we surrender the impulse and cast ourselves onto God each time it shows its ugly head, we receive the power to be free of it. And gradually, the impulses themselves get fewer and farther between. Healing.

When taking Steps Six and Seven for the first time, our thought may typically be, That's a good idea; why not? And we go ahead and ask that all or at least such-and-such defects be removed—resentment, for example. But later, when the flames of resentment begin to consume us again, we may finally despair of it enough to really work the Steps on it. By then, we're ready to say, I'm ready for You to take them *all* away!

These realizations may come about gradually or in a moment of what seems like suicidal surrender of our destructive self.

Some of us may experience sudden release from some defects, but for most of us there is one practical way to overcome our wrongs that has never failed: We surrender them up to God and *practice* making them right. After all, how much practice did it take to burn these sick patterns into our brains and souls?

If we have a habit of lying or fudging the truth, we undo it by correcting the lie with the person involved. If we're resentful or hostile, we undo it by going to the person affected and admitting where we've been wrong. Where the other party is not overtly affected, we overcome the resentment by surrendering it and praying for that person. Or, we may find we even have to tell that person about it to break its power over us, provided it doesn't injure them or others.

> *"It was in Step-study meetings where I learned how others were actually getting victory over their resentment. I was told to pray for the person I resented, asking for him or her what I wanted for myself, not just once, but every time I thought of that person. Even when I didn't feel like it; and*

> *I never do. It really works. I don't know if it does them any good, but it sure keeps me from burning up with it."*

We find it helpful to pray for the objects of our lust because we're making the wrong right. The wrong within us, the negative force that lust represents, gets turned into a positive force inside as we give out to that person instead of taking in. Giving out heals *us*. We make the decision not to resort to lust, surrendering it up to God, and *then* He gives us the power to be free of it.

A Loving God Who Knows and Cares

As we glimpse the true nature of our spiritual and moral bankruptcy, we can only wonder what kind of God this is who can not only stand to see and know it all, but who patiently and mercifully works in us and with us toward turning these dreadful liabilities into song. God is surely for the sexaholic.

One member's experience presents a deeply personal perspective on these Steps:

> I was twenty, in school, and just married to the first girl I'd ever dated. What a transition for a practicing sexaholic!
>
> Sex with a woman was new and wonderful. What a relief. I'd never have to resort to sex with myself again. Rude awakening! Within weeks I was doing it. Again! Why? Sex in the marriage was perfect. The confusion forced me to see a counselor for help.
>
> The session went well. We had a nice conversation about everything but why I was really there. I couldn't bring myself to talk about my masturbation problem. It was too shameful. What I did instead was finally blurt out, "Do you know so-and-so at school?" mentioning another person by name. "I think he masturbates, and isn't that terrible!"

The counselor looked at me oddly but said nothing, and I walked out of there feeling dim relief, until only hours later, when I went on another lust-sex binge.

I had practically forgotten that incident until some time into sexual sobriety. I was working on a new Fourth Step inventory and put the man I had wronged on my amends list. When I finally found him—thirty-four years later—he was thrilled to hear from me. Until I told him why I was calling.

As I related what I had done, I was overcome with guilt and shame. It descended on me with such clarity and force that I wanted to dash madly away from myself. But there was nowhere left to go. I had to "walk through" my feelings. This led me to write a mini-inventory on the matter, and only then did I discover what had really happened. In the counselor's office thirty-four years before, instead of acknowledging my own problem, I had transferred it onto another. I hadn't even known the fellow and had no idea what he was doing.

But I needed someone to bear my shame and guilt. Anyone! It was crushing me, and I couldn't stand it anymore. So I tried to get rid of it on someone else. And it worked—for a time. It kept me from looking at myself. Of course I had no idea that I would have to keep on finding scapegoats again and again and again to transfer my wrongfulness onto others.

The easiest targets were my own wife and children. Now I see why they could "never do anything right" and why I was always finding fault. I had to. I needed to transfer my wrongs continually to keep from seeing what *I* really was on the inside. The rest of the world didn't fare any better. The boss was an idiot, fellow workers were inferior types, the President, Governor, neighbors, brothers and sisters, institutions. . . . I was letting my negative force out on everyone and everything I could safely do it to, especially those within my own circle of nearness.

I see now that what I was doing was yet another natural instinct gone astray. I *can't* bear my own wrongs; they destroy me. But I have to have someone bear them or I'll die. But no one can. Even if they want to, they can't. I had been looking in the wrong place.

After learning, through the fellowship of the program, to turn my will and my life over to the care of God by trial and error, I had come to see that it really worked. All my emotional, spiritual, physical, and material needs were being met, one day at a time. The question now was, *Could I turn my wrongs over to Him too?* Instead of making others bear them or bear them myself in self-destructive depression or resorting to a succession of other "drugs" to cover them, could *He* bear them for me so I wouldn't have to? Could He take them away?

I tried it. Every time I surrendered a wrong in process—temptation to lust, resentment, or fear, for example—and would say something to the effect, "I don't want to bear this; I want You to bear it for me; I cast it onto You," it worked. *Someone* has to bear my wrong, and Someone does. I can't conceive of such a provision for *me*, but I accept it. All I know is that whenever and on whatever defect I take this action, it has never failed.

Steps Eight and Nine

"Made a list of all persons we had harmed, and became willing to make amends to them all."

"Made direct amends to such people wherever possible, except when to do so would injure them or others."

The Indelible List

We've always had this list inside us; it was burned into our brains. That was the problem. We kept pushing it under, covering it over, drugging it, running from it, or trying to sex it out of existence. But those names, faces, and scenes just kept coming back to haunt us. And the more we pretended we were not blameworthy, the more wrong we did and the longer the list grew!

Little did we realize that every wrong was adding to *our* burden of guilt and distress and creating more illness. We could not wish or will the guilt away. Only when we stopped running, when we turned around and looked them full in the face and set about making them right, was their power over us broken. *That's* when we were set free.

"I never worked these Steps because I couldn't see what was in it for me. Now I see that every one of

> *those jobs I did on people made a dark hole inside me. And I've been draining away out of those holes!"*

Now we see that the amends process is a healing one—for us! The damage we've done to ourselves *can* be healed. We surrender our ego, pride, and fear and go to it.

If our Fourth and Fifth Steps were thorough, names probably popped out at us at every turn, and we made note of these at the time. Now, we simply draw them all together into a single list, writing down what we did wrong next to each name. In addition, some may want to jot down names of people that keep coming to mind with negative feelings associated with them. Most often, such memories are signals from the subconscious that we have unfinished business there too.

Some of us wanted to jump into making our amends, often as compulsively as we worked our habit. But we found it wise to discuss the list with our sponsor before taking any action, especially where spouse, children, and former lovers were involved. This was a safeguard for us and the others in several ways. The sponsor could see better than we whether we were merely trying to dump our guilt or were sincerely trying to undo the wrong and make it right. He or she could tell whether we were emotionally ready to confront these people and could do so honestly, without reminding them of their wrongs. If the amends had to do with money or property, the sponsor helped us see what was involved. Sometimes we also needed help to see which amends took priority and which could wait for a better time. The sponsor helped us assess the impact it might have on the wronged party. And above all, the sponsor was able to sense whether we had forgiven the injured party for any wrongs they had done to us.

Step "Eight and One-Half"

This brings up a very important matter—forgiveness. Often, we perceive that the ones we have wronged are themselves guilty of real or imagined wrongs against us. Nursing these resentments, we had never forgiven them.

> *"I was petrified because I resented those people and didn't have the words for amends. God gave me the words when the time was right and when I was right."*

Somewhere between making the list and making the amends, there's an unwritten requirement that we forgive. (Although there seem to be times when we have to make the amends *before* we can forgive.) And we discover we're as powerless over resentment and an unforgiving spirit as we ever were over lust, sex, or dependency. So what do we do? We work the Steps on it, as on everything else.

> *"I just had to admit, 'Hey, I don't want to forgive him.' Regardless of how I tried, I just could not bring myself to feel forgiving. So I just admitted this to God and the group. When I heard that everyone else had the same trouble, I could admit I was powerless over it, do a Step One, Two, and Three on it, and give it up to God. Then I just asked for the willingness to take the action anyway, first in my heart. And it wasn't long before I could hear myself in my mind saying, 'Dad, I forgive you.' And I was overwhelmed; I felt the forgiveness flow, and I was released."*

We take the action of forgiving, even when we don't feel forgiving. Most of us never seem to feel forgiving until we take that inner action of giving up our right to resent. Practicing forgiveness in our hearts as we think of these people, then aloud, perhaps even with our sponsor, we forgive every person on our list and keep on forgiving them every time the resentment returns. We may find it necessary to forgive and pray for them each time we think about them until we are free of the resentment. The willingness and the gift of love do come if we persist.

What is resentment but a conscious decision to turn against someone, a separation? It is thus an inner anger, a distortion of the truth, a lie used to cover our own wrong. Resentment and its companions, hostility and anger, are not only one of the universal hallmarks of our spiritual malady but, unsurrendered, are one of our greatest liabilities.

Why forgive? For us it is very simple. If we don't forgive, we're never free. Unless we forgive, *we* are not forgiven; we remain chained to our wrongs, unable to free ourselves, leave the dark dungeon of our past, and walk in the sunlight of love.

If we are to give this aspect of our program its due, we should give it special emphasis:

> *"Surrendering our resentments, we asked for willingness to forgive all persons guilty of real or imagined wrongs against us and forgave each one."*

Step Nine

Once we took the actions of forgiving others, we were free to start making amends. We read pertinent sections in *Alcoholics Anonymous* and the *Twelve and Twelve* for valuable guidance and stayed close to our sponsors as we prayerfully made one amends after another until we had done absolutely all we could to undo each wrong without injuring that person or others.

There is always some way to make an amends, even when the injured person is dead, lost, or nameless. One can find those in need to whom indirect amends can be made. Of course, this should never take the place of direct amends, wherever such are possible. Some members, for example, have made amends to the prostitutes they had abetted in their destructive way of life by praying for every one they see on the streets and for those in their past that come to mind. Some have made monetary amends for past pilfering on the job by working voluntary unpaid overtime, when making direct amends might have injured their own family. For those of us who have abused wives, husbands, or children, the amends must begin with a sexually sober changed attitude and behavior on a daily basis. Then, as we grow in recovery, we will find how to make more direct amends. Help from sponsor and group is indispensable here. There's always a way, if we really want to make things right.

There's no feeling in all the world like having mended a long-standing wrong. It is better than the relief that comes from finally pulling a thorn from a festering finger, more like pulling a thorn from our festering soul. Soul surgery. By the grace of God, we make ourselves well, and the healing process spreads to those about us. It is an adventure of the highest order. Often experiencing anxiety, with the adrenalin running high, we come to life. It is the moment of truth. We cast ourselves onto God. We courageously come face to face, not only with that other person we've avoided, but with ourselves—the real monster we've been fleeing all our lives. Then, when we've done it, there's a marvelous sense of accomplishment: release, relief, and great joy. Why did we ever wait so long?

A note of caution: Here again we suggest that newcomers to Sexaholics Anonymous *not* reveal their sexual past to a spouse or family member who does not already know of it without careful consideration and a period of sexual sobriety, and even then, not without prior discussion with an SA sponsor or group. Typically, when we come into the program, we want to share our excitement with those closest to us and tell all right away. Such disclosures might injure our family or others and should be confined to the group of which we are a part until a wise course is indicated. Of course, if there is any chance we have put others in danger, we take immediate steps to try to correct that.

Few things can so damage the possibility of healing in the family as a *premature* confession to spouse or family where sacred bonds and trust have been violated. Unwittingly, such confessions can be attempts on our part to dump our guilt, get back into good graces, or make just another show of willpower.

Step Ten

"Continued to take personal inventory and when we were wrong promptly admitted it."

"I was wrong . . ." Between two people, these are the most beautiful words in the world.

We were great at saying, "I love you, I need you, I want you." It was easy. The words often gushed out on a flood of fuzzy feelings—straight out of our sickness. But these other three little words, admitting our wrong, are the hardest words in all the world to say. Why?

Why were they the words we demanded from others but could never give? Why is it that of all the Twelve Steps, the making of amends to another is the most difficult and least followed? Why is it that so many of us, even those experienced in the Twelve Step program—often very articulate and with years of sobriety—can never bring ourselves to say these words?

Is it because these words strike hardest at our egos? Is it because they force us to the level of the other person and threaten to place us beneath them? Is it because they expose us at our weakest, for what we really are, rendering us vulnerable and without defense? Is it because the barrier these words would break down is not only the barrier we have built up between ourselves and the other person, but by that very token also the barrier between ourselves and God? (Otherwise, why do we feel cut off from God while harboring an uncorrected wrong?) Is it because in order for us to confess our wrong to others, we must first be willing to forgive them? And who can forgive? Forgiving another is as divine an act as we humans can ever aspire to. It's as hard or harder to say "I forgive you" as it is to admit wrong. But we can and must forgive!

The highest reach of the soul is outward toward another in this motion of reconciliation. This Step is the great maker of true spiritual union. What better chance to forge true union than in the heat of misunderstanding, wrong, acknowledgment of wrong, and forgiveness? There is no greater bond than the one issuing from such atonement. It welds people at the very heart of their being—where they hurt the most. If we wish to recover from our dread isolation, there is no other way. And is not this how we make our union with God? This spiritual encounter is at the sacred interface between one person's heart and another, the very same sanctuary where we meet our Maker. It is here, where we are willing to lose ourselves and humble ourselves before one another. At-one-ment. There is no holier ground.

What power there is in such union, this fellowship of the forgiven who are forgiving one another! It is the grand equation for the release of Life. If we have this power of love for one another, it will be irresistible!

Sober Is Not Well

There is something wrong with the person who cannot make a straight, honest, unequivocal amends. If this is true of us, we suspect it is because we are not fully surrendered. That attitude of self-obsession underlying our spiritual illness still lingers. And most of us fit into this category. We are as powerless over this inability to make a clean amends as we ever were over lust, sex, or dependency. That's why we have to do it, *because* it doesn't come naturally! We don't feel like making amends, but we do it, and the feelings follow. If we find we are not yet willing to make the amends, we go back to Steps One, Two, and Three, admit our powerlessness, surrender our pride, and cast ourselves onto God and others for help.

It is possible that, once relieved of the compulsion to act out our habit, we may feel cured and start coasting along with our tank on EMPTY. But the same personality defects that energized our addiction are still with us and, unattended, will take their toll again, sooner or later. Why are they still with us? Because they *are* us. Progressive victory *over* these defects, not their eradication, is the power of God at work in us. What we really do battle against is not other people but our old natures, the negative force within us we can obey anytime we wish, the force that is always willing and able to wrong another. This is why our program must come to fruition in our daily living or there is no recovery.

A Program for Living

"Continued . . ." The simple wisdom of that one word. The essence of this Step—and this program—is a continuing *process*. These spiritual principles are a way of sound living, not merely some one-time technique for kicking a habit. We replace the addictive process with a process of recovery and growth. Step Ten is thus a continuation of the moral inventory of Steps Four and Five, the surrendering of our wrongs in Steps Six and Seven, and the righting of our wrongs in Steps Eight and Nine, all based on our personal surrender in Steps One, Two, and Three and done on a daily basis in the workaday world of everyday living.

Daily living is the arena in which this program finds its true mettle tested. For it is as we encounter

> The slings and arrows of outrageous fortune . . .
> The heart-ache, and the thousand natural shocks
> That flesh is heir to

that we see what we are made of and recognize our great need. Our relations with others are the touchstone. Thus, the spouse, the children, the parents and siblings, the boss, the fellow workers, and our fellow program members all represent the greatest potential sources for conflict and emotional distress as well as the greatest opportunity for applying these principles and creating union and healing.

> *"Making amends seems to be what gives me the most practice in changing my defects of character. It makes me think twice before opening my big mouth, knowing how painful the prospect of making amends will be."*

A New Habit

We are needy people. Our self-obsession leads the way, taking pride and resentment hand in hand, with fear, doubt, dishonesty, and all our other uglies following close behind. We need continually to see ourselves as we really are and others as they really are. We need continually to correct our wrong attitudes and actions with respect to the other people in our lives. We need to learn how to restore relationship and find union. Thus, we need to learn a new habit—taking continued personal inventory.

Instead of looking always and only at others, we start looking at ourselves. We had always lived for ourselves; now we *look* at ourselves. This is a program of self-examination, which develops slowly in the process of attending meetings, making mistakes, doing wrong, learning to see and acknowledge our wrongs, and correcting those wrongs. This is why in practice, so many have incorporated daily writing as part of working the Tenth Step, as discussed in the *Twelve and Twelve* and Chapter 6 of *Alcoholics Anonymous*. Also, we sit down after an emotional scene, for example, and ask ourselves, Why am *I* disturbed? Where was *I* wrong? What did *I* do or fail to do that makes me feel this way? How can *I* correct it? This kind of writing can work wonders.

Step Ten is the Step we work anywhere and everywhere we interact with people, especially at home, at work, and in meetings. That's where the action is, where life is, where people are, and where our cunning, baffling, and powerful egos are. We work it promptly, on the spot, as close to the heat of the action as we can. There is no faster, no better, no other way to get well.

"I'm the Key"

The following story is one member's experience that illustrates the change of attitude that is the key to this most-important amends-making principle of our program.

> I had finally had it with my wife. She had to get help to change herself—or else! Married to her for years and now sober, I guess I knew when she was all loused up. I had her diagnosed as a television addict, rebellious, blind to seeing herself, and powerless to change. The description sounded disturbingly familiar, but I was too sure of myself to think it could ever apply to me. I had her nailed and felt pretty strongly about the whole thing. It was an ultimatum: Shape up or ship out.
>
> I left for the weekend on a fishing trip with another sexaholic to get away from the whole situation. On the way home, finally talking freely about our identical problems, the light dawned. *I* was the key, and my attitude was wrong.
>
> I was waiting for *her* to change, not realizing that my very attitude made that impossible. The woman is united to me. Good or bad, she is united to me—spiritually. I don't understand this, but when my attitude is negative, rejecting, censorious, she is united to my spiritual illness.
>
> I saw that if God had waited for me to shape up before He began working for my recovery and healing, I'd still be lost or dead. When I was still defective was when He was doing the most to call me back. I see this now, looking back on the whole thing. He was patiently leading me out years before I had even the slightest

self-awareness and honesty. At my lowest, He was leading with His most magnificent selfless love—for *me*, in spite of my wrong, *because* I was defective and powerless.

And this, I discovered on that road back from the lake, was how I was to treat and love my wife; not as *wife*, but as another person in the program, whether she was or not! I was to treat her as God and others had been treating *me*. As my SA friend and I drove back from those honest hours together, my attitude changed.

And in returning, I could tell from her first response to me—that first cautious glance—that she responded to my change in attitude toward her. She sensed it; unspoken, she knew it. And just as suddenly as I had changed, so did she.

I could feel it. My negative had changed to embrace her, whatever she was. And whatever she was *changed*!

The woman is united to me. I don't understand this. But now, instead of being united to my resentment, fault-finding, and condemning-rejecting spirit, she's united to my own healing.

I don't want to be, but I'm the key. What I *am* is what I get, and the measure I give is the measure I get back. I pray God for the willingness to take up this key and unlock the door to love.

Step Eleven

"Sought through prayer and meditation to improve our conscious contact with God as we understood Him, praying only for knowledge of His will for us and the power to carry that out."

A Faith That Works

Improve our contact with God? When did we ever have any real contact? Along our journey through Steps One through Ten, unless we were fooling ourselves. Our admission of powerlessness should have been surrender to God. Our change of attitude resulted in commitment of our lives to God. The moral inventory was our admission of what we really were to God. Those thousands of "telegrams" for help—getting moment-by-moment relief from our obsession and defects—was resorting to God instead of to self. And atonement with those we had hurt and estranged marvelously opened the way for restored union with God.

Little did we realize that in taking all these actions for survival, sobriety, and serenity, we were finding our God! So long as we held on to our lusts, He was lost to us. But now, with our having torn down the wall of our wrongs, with nothing between, there He was, within.

> "Ah, fondest, blindest, weakest,
> I am He whom thou seekest! . . ."
>
> (Francis Thompson)

How fortunate we are, then, to be so needy that we have to find what our lust was really looking for—the loving God who is our refuge and our strength.

Striving after God is as natural as breathing. Most of mankind has been praying from the beginning; man has been called "the praying animal." The problem was not God; there was something wrong with *us*. Our wrongs had separated us, not from praying to God (many of us did that ad nauseam), but from *union* with our God. As a result, our concept of God was wrong, and we were lost to the true God. He was either an avenging tyrant we were afraid to approach, the great Authority Figure, a Santa Claus, or some other reflection of our distorted attitudes and dysfunctional relationships. We acted as though "being good" (not acting out) somehow earned us the right to "be bad" (act out). We were trying to manipulate or make deals with God like we did with others! Creating a god to suit our sickness. And if we snagged the brass ring on the merry-go-round once in a while, we were superstitious enough to believe our way and our kind of god was working, enough to keep pulling us on for another free whirl. Some of us never got the brass ring—and some of us didn't care whether there was a brass ring or not—but kept on endlessly paying the price of admission anyway.

No wonder it never worked for us. And no wonder that what we really wanted was to fill the great void at the center of our being and to have a faith that worked.

What Kind of God?

With little regard for who He is or His will for us, we insisted on trying to use God for our own selfish ends, which only kept us from seeing what we really were and who He really is. Thus, with all the false gods we clung to—lust, sex, the body of a man or woman, other people in our dependency, things, pleasure, food, work, money, success—some of us still instinctively went through our religious exercises, of whatever persuasion they might have been, lost to what was on the other side of our idolatry.

But what if God was *for* us, not as we saw ourselves, but as we truly were? What if He saw us with all our wrongs and made Himself one with us in providing for our release? If this were true, we could bring God into our wrongs! And we who were absolutely without power over our wrongs could be freed from their power every time we gave them up to God.

Have we not seen this in our own experience? Each time when we are faced with temptation from within or without, and we surrender, are we not freed from its power? Whenever we fulfill this simple condition we are saved from acting out our wrong. No matter that we may not know *how* God is doing it. That it is His victory and not ours is obvious, considering our inability to save ourselves.

The Natural Connection

If this be true, how fortunate we are to have so clear and continuing a need for calling on such a God for release, guidance, and peace. How precious a privilege to be in His sphere of influence, under His guidance, if indeed we have become reconciled to Him in those first nine Steps. And how natural it is for such a one to pray.

Just as surely as air is the breath of life for our bodies, prayer becomes the breath of life for our spirits. It is the means by which we make our Connection. Just as talking to another in the fellowship of forgiveness is the medium of life between people, so prayer as the expression of our inner being is the means by which we have fellowship with God. And it is just as natural! This is why we must learn to walk in the light and have fellowship with one another and why the right kind of meetings is so important. Right fellowship with others is of the same order as right fellowship with

God. If we say we have the latter without the former, we are not true.

Thus, prayer becomes not so much a matter of asking for something as it is a means of life and growth of the inner person . Prayer and meditation meet at this point; they both offer the means of union with our God. Fulfillment, peace, and rest.

While meditation in the narrower sense is a quieting and opening of the inner person to God, prayer is what we voice audibly or inwardly when we are in *any* condition, place, or time. Often, prayer and meditation become one.

> *"I'll do it when I feel a need for help. Say resentment has struck again, or when I'm in a stressful or tempting situation, or when I feel that great emptiness inside. I reach out for the presence of God, saying, 'I reach out for your presence right now.' I hold my mind steady on His presence as being with me and as being in that situation. The problem fades away. It's as though I'm lifted onto a plane that rises above it, and I feel that oneness again."*

Learning how to pray in sobriety is like learning how to walk or talk; no one can tell us how or do it for us. We learn by doing, like everything else in this program. We just start talking to God.

Noisy Souls

Most of us coming into Sexaholics Anonymous seem to have our inner being filled with noise much of the time. Pollution. We may not be aware of this at first, since it has built up gradually over the years and we don't sense it as abnormal. Increasingly we became more dependent on filling our eyes and ears (and mouths?) with "noise." It permeates our modern world as a constant barrage of sensory inputs of every imaginable sort.

Being what we are—addicts—this has become part of our illness. It seems unnatural to be without it. When we go somewhere to "get away from it all," we usually take it with us in some form or other. The world's supply is always out there beguiling and "entertaining" us with "different," "better," and "more." This noise helps distract us from our own spiritual discord—a noise all its own—and also feeds this discord. *Anything* to keep us from feeling our feelings and seeing what we are inside. Anything to keep us from resorting to the water of life that alone fully satisfies.

This is why when we stop our acting-out and come off our primary drug, we may feel uneasy, anxious, or wired.

> *"I've never been able to stand still. My whole life I've been running. I can't be alone with myself. The best I could start out with in sobriety was just a simple prayer, and even that was usually on the run. I had to get into this prayer and meditation thing like a little baby, one faltering step at a time."*

Meditation

Who knows what are all the effects of the incessant artificial stimulation present in today's environment? Meditation has proven to be not only beneficial to mind and body but one of the best natural methods of quieting our inner disturbance. These results can appear in meditation even apart from any prayer or religious association.

For us however, meditation without working the first ten Steps can thwart the achievement of the intended result and defeat its purpose. If we meditate without prior surrender of our will and lives to God, what will we be connected to? Without facing our own wrongs, how can our inner eye see aright? And without an attitude of wanting to right our wrongs, how can we hope to know the Good? Some of us have had the experience that when "in the wrong place," we can, in meditation, actually connect with the dark side of ourselves. After all, we get back a reflection of what we really are.

However else we work the Steps, there is benefit in working them in order.

Step Eleven in the *Twelve and Twelve* provides a practical introduction on how to start meditating for those who have never done it. The following is one SA member's experience:

> I usually begin the day by reading a passage from program or devotional literature or Scripture. I ask God to keep me sober for that day from my lust, resentment, and other negative emotions, citing the defects that have been raising their heads lately and giving me trouble.
>
> It doesn't work if I'm holding on to resentment or an unforgiving attitude; my mind will drift and focus on others in a negative way, and I'll have to stop. It also doesn't work for me if my mind is full of media images from the previous day or evening.
>
> Then I meditate, using a passage or phrase that sticks in my mind. Or, I might use the Lord's name or a phrase from the Twenty-Third Psalm or the Lord's Prayer. Repetition aloud helps me quiet down, and often I'll find myself repeating it inwardly. I've gone through stages where different passages or ways of addressing God are more meaningful to me at a particular time in my life. As I quiet down, I often experience the gentle peace of oneness and union. It gets better over the years, but there are dry times when I seem to have to back off and not push it. These may indicate I need to do some work on myself.
>
> Often, during meditation, other people will come to mind, and I'll pray for them, or I'll pray that God will bring His kingdom to come into some area or enterprise, that His will be done in it.
>
> During the day, if I'm in stress or trouble or anxiety, I'll get alone somewhere and have a mini-medi-

tation for a few minutes, or as long as I can spare. It has never failed to bring me peace.

Meditation is an indicator of what we really are on the inside. It will reveal whether the channel is open, clear, clean, and quiet. Often it is not; but that's how we learn. And it's a progressive thing. Slowly we try it, first for just a few minutes, then longer as we discover what it does for us.

The essence of Step Eleven is *letting God in* through every temptation, emotion, difficulty, success, failure, sadness, and joy. True union with the Source of our lives.

Step Twelve

> *"Having had a spiritual awakening as the result of these Steps, we tried to carry this message to sexaholics and practice these principles in all our affairs."*

This is the Step that doesn't need to be written and can't be made to happen. It is the inevitable *result* of what has already happened. If a person is experiencing the reality of Steps One through Eleven, he or she is manifesting the truth of that new life.

Staying sober is our initial objective; a spiritual awakening is the unintended result. If our experience tells us anything, it is that there is no *healing* without such an awakening. And the difference between merely not acting out our addiction (being "dry") and healing is the new life. If we want the old life intact, simply minus the habit, we don't really want healing, for our sickness *is* the old way of life.

The Awakening

What is "the result of these Steps"? It is the surrender of Step One to the reality of our powerlessness, that we are sexaholics and our own way is not working. It is commitment to God as the one who can restore us to sanity (Two and Three). It is the ability to see and disclose to another the true nature of what we really are (Four and Five). It is giving up all those defects of which we become aware and asking God to take them (Six and Seven). It is a desire to right all our wrongs (Eight, Nine, and Ten). And it is conscious union with the true Source of our lives (Eleven). An awakening to Life.

The result of working the Steps is not primarily a physical or emotional awakening, though these are involved. It is essentially a spiritual awakening, where the spirit that was dead to God, others, and rightness is made alive to God, alive to others, and alive to rightness. Spiritual awakening is not mere sobriety, an awakening to knowledge about the Steps, belief in the Steps, or psychological insights into why they work. It is a change of state, an awakening of what was once dead.

The Message

The awakening is accompanied by an impulse to share it with others, right from the very start. That impulse arises spontaneously from within the recovering heart: "I want to give away what I've got. I *have* to give away what I've got." We must be very clear about what the real message is that we carry. Listen to how one member puts it:

> *"The only thing I can bear witness to is the truth of my own experience. Because that's what I want to hear from others. I want to see and feel the real truth about someone's inner life and behavior that I can identify with. I don't want to be told or preached at. Knowing the truth about religion or the program didn't do it for me. Coming to see and acknowledge the truth about myself is what got me through the door into this new way of life. It's the truth about myself—the imperfect truth—that attracts others; not all the preaching in the world."*

If we're still alive to our old way of life, dead toward God, and dead in our wrongs, the message we carry is illness and death. Sober or not sober, even if the words coming out of our mouths are perfectly true, we cannot communicate *life*. If we have died to our wrongs and are alive to God, the message we carry is life, even if the words coming out of our mouths are few, unlearned, or halting.

Life gives birth to life. We *want* others to recover. Another paradox in the spiritual realm is that if we don't give it away, we can't keep it. We learn to practice becoming open to the needs of others, being generous with ourselves.

Practicing the Principles

The end of Step Twelve, "and practiced these principles in all our affairs," is not the end but the beginning for us. By its very nature, our recovery must go beyond the mere cessation of our acting out. Lust and dependency are more than sick externals; they strike at the very soul of our connection with God and others and have corroded the very heart of our humanity. That heart is what must be renewed. If we are to give this aspect of our program its due, we should give it special emphasis: call it Step "Twelve and One-Half."

> *"Took the actions of love to improve our relations with others."*

Accentuate the Positive

Negative sobriety didn't work. It was uncomfortable, dangerous, and short-lived.

> *"I was not cheating on my wife. I was not having sex with myself. I was not looking at the pictures or going to those places. Not, not, not. . . For months and months I was NOT. Until one day, NOT was not enough, and I went back out there."*

We discovered that unless we found what our lust was trying so unsuccessfully to fill, we were not going to make it. Either we filled the vacuum with the real thing or we had nothing but the negative. Either we started practicing the actions of love or we wound up headed back into that futile fabrication we called "making love."

Also, we found that improving our conscious union with God was impossible without improving our conscious union with others. Both relations were broken together and both had to be healed together. It was the only way that brought us peace. We could not have one without the other. We who did not truly love wife or husband or children or parents or brother or sister, whom we could see, could not love God whom we could not see.

Healing for us is incomplete without the positive sobriety of healed relations with others. Often we see that our relational poverty and malfunctions began in childhood in a dysfunctional environment. After we are sober and in recovery for awhile, many of us begin to feel the need for looking at and working on this neglected area of our lives.

Doing What Comes Un-Naturally

"Love" is one of the most abused words in the language. That's why we speak not of loving but of taking the *actions* of love. Just as with faith, love, we discovered, was not a feeling, but attitude in action. We took the actions we knew we should be taking toward others *because* we did not feel like it. The feelings followed. Love for us is *doing*—doing what does *not* come naturally.

> *"Even though I knew I had to break out of myself, look at my wife, and smile, I just knew I couldn't. I don't know why. But if I simply did it, the feeling of wanting to followed."*

We start going to meetings and participating in the fellowship of the program before we feel we want to. We stop sexing, lusting, and resenting before we feel we can. And we start taking the right actions toward others before we feel like doing them naturally. This is the paradox of this "impossible" program.

How can we do this when we feel so powerless and aren't sure we even want to? We have a God who works, that's why; His business is raising us out of our death! But "faith without action is dead." We receive that power *as we take the action*, not before.

> *"A hundred such incidents and I was beginning to learn that the key to doing what did not come naturally was surrender, the key to this whole program. The key to my own happiness. When I distrust my own feelings and just go ahead and do what's right, the miracle happens and I'm out of my dark hole."*

Many of us discovered that once these actions become customary and incorporated in our day-to-day living, we actually begin to *change*. We become better people and, as a result, happier with ourselves and others.

Giving up the "Gimmies"

In previous Steps we became aware of how our natural tendency was to take from others, using them as inputs to our lives, much as we used food, drink, or entertainment. Now, we start learning how to recognize and surrender this "natural" impulse, deny ourselves the right to misuse anyone, and start *giving* of ourselves with no thought of getting anything in return except our own peace of mind and freedom. "The measure we give is the measure we get back."

> *"When the grass looks greener on the other side of the fence, I start watering my own lawn."*

> *"At first, what gave me the most practice in giving was encountering lust objects. I grew to realize that in drinking in the fantasy-intensified image of that person, I was* taking. *With or without their consent, through that look of lust, I was taking something violently from that person. I* had *them.*

> *So, I began praying for every one my eyes wanted to snatch. At first it seemed impossible; I felt like doing that about as much as. . . But as soon as I did it, not only did the lust vanish, but I felt this great release. I'd say anything, like 'Please help her,' just so it was going* out *of me instead of my pulling her into me. It satisfied! Lusting never did. Where had I been all this time?"*

We are filled in the giving. We are fed as we deal out our bread to another. It's not in advance or for more than one event at a time.

All along, this is what we had really been looking for, lusting for, sexing for, and taking for. By taking, we had separated ourselves from others, ourselves, and God. By giving, we found true union with others and God, and, lo and behold, love itself. But it slipped in unrecognized through the back door. "Surprised by joy."

True Union

We saw that the truth revealed in the *Twelve and Twelve* applied squarely to us: "The primary fact that we fail to recognize is our total inability to form a true partnership with another human being." (p. 53)

The great love "makers" were really love cripples all along and didn't know it. Sex partners were little more than targets to be scored, materialized fantasies to be tracked down, captured, possessed, and sooner or later discarded. In romantic relationships sex was complicated with lust or unhealthy dependency. Often spouses, in addition to being sex objects, were also parent figures and objects of dependency. So what were our chances of learning how to relate normally to anyone when the heart of our relational apparatus was so out of kilter?

We found that we were just as powerless over trying to relate rightly to others as we had been in putting down our habit; it was *part of* our habit. Thus, we had to approach it the same way, using the Steps—the miracle-workers. When we did, we could literally watch ourselves grow into true manhood and womanhood.

To illustrate, the story below reveals some of the changes one sexaholic went through in his marriage in the first several years of sobriety. This is the same member whose introduction to sobriety appears in the personal story at the beginning of this book. Single members have shared that they identify; the same principles apply in all human relations.

Just the Beginning

I began going to meetings and came off my physical drugs: sex, alcohol, tranquilizers. Then I began coming off the first of my spiritual drugs—lust. From the wife I expected immediate, warm, overflowing gratitude and acceptance. After all, I was now sober, good, and true, wasn't I? The response I got was NOTHING!

I kept waiting for her to enfold me with love and care. I expected her response to be as great as my newfound experience. Nothing! The ingrate! I thought. Can't you see what I'm giving up for you?! Resentment flared toward her for not understanding what I was going through. That got me less than nothing!

After a few weeks, then months of sobriety, she and the boy were *still* doing everything wrong. And I was back to acting toward them like I'd always acted—irritable, flying off the handle at the slightest thing, rejecting. Sober!

Sobriety did bring one important change: whenever my anger or resentment surged, instead of using it as an excuse to go sex out, I'd use it as an excuse to escape out. But the back door still got it every time. WHAM! I'd go to a movie or just drive into the city to get rid of that awful feeling of inner pressure, a kind of claustrophobia. Driving or walking around the city streets was my old pattern. I just knew I had to get away from THEM.

Scenes with the wife and boy continued in sobriety. Such scenes seemed to be the only way I knew to relate on an intimate level. (Seems our sex was not really *relating* at all; just part of the illness! What a shock.) Each big blowup was the END. "Finished!" "This is IT!" "I can't take this any more!" This lasted for *years*, but the incidents gradually got to be less often.

Somehow I learned to leave just after the battle got started, and eventually before it got under way. I discovered that escaping to a meeting or to my sponsor's house was better than going "out there." Progress.

More of the same, only I stopped slamming the door. Most of the time.

I launched a program of trying to get my wife to go to Twelve Step meetings so she would change, with or without me. Nothing! "I don't need those meetings" was the short response. "*You* do!" More resentment and escape.

The Sunday morning "talks." Me to her. "It's very important for me to talk with you now," I'd say. It doesn't register that she's less than enthusiastic—*dread* would be a better word. Turns out the talks are really monologues (How did she ever stand it so long?), my trying to manipulate and convince her what's wrong with *her*. Only now I'm doing it with "kindness." Well, I wasn't yelling as much, anyway. "Can't you see? . . ." I'd keep telling her. Looking back on it, I get the strange feeling I was doing the same thing I'd been doing in the psychiatrist's office or group therapy: egorrhea—diarrhea of the ego. And whenever she'd try and express herself, I'd get angry and stomp off.

It took *years* for this pattern to change; that was all we knew! But she slowly became gun-shy of those "talks." Turns out I was simply unable/unwilling to look at myself, though she did force me to peek inside once in a while. (Maybe the program was giving me a little honesty.) Then I'd have to go to a meeting or see my sponsor right afterward, the pain was so bad. I didn't know it was the healthy pain of self-awareness creeping in; I just knew it was IMPOSSIBLE TO LIVE WITH THAT WOMAN! Now, I thank God for her courage and honesty and patience, and the boy's. God's gift to me. Pure grace.

A few years into sobriety, instead of the marriage getting better, it seemed to be getting worse. And the beautiful light that had shone in her face at the beginning of our marriage continued to fade, the joy and song dried up and blown away across the desert of our desperation. In sobriety!

The close encounters of the nasty kind became less frequent but seemed more final. Time after time, we both went away with the feeling that there was no possible solution.

Then she began to see the pattern. Whenever I was in "that mood," I'd apparently try to put it off on her with an attack. Usually some tremendous issue, like hair in the washbasin. Earth-shattering. Turns out what was really at work was my cunning, baffling, and powerful lust looking for an excuse to change partners. No wonder every once in a while I'd have fantasies of her dying.

Somehow, she began to see that she was not the cause of my moods, that there was something else behind these attacks on her that had nothing to do with her or her "transgressions." Important discovery. She began to confront me with this, but I'd close off or strike out all the more. I now see that what I was doing was transferring my own wrongfulness onto another so I wouldn't have to bear it.

As it dawned on her that I had been attacking her to cover what I was and what I had been doing, her anger and resentment flared to white heat.

It's important to note the time scale here, and the pain scale. Years. And yelling, running, and walking through loads of pain. Years and pain—that's what it took for us.

The pain got so bad for me that I had no choice but to start working the principles embodied in our Steps. And that's when things started slowly turning around. *Mere sobriety, even lengthy sobriety, hadn't healed me or the marriage!* Going to meetings? Big deal! I had to start seeing and changing *me*, or the pain would keep returning and the marriage keep dissolving. I was like the man the alcoholics talk about who, every time he went through a certain doorway, got hit over the head with a two-by-four. But he'd still keep on going through that same doorway! The brick wall syndrome: if you run up against a brick wall, keep battering it with your head. Finally, I got sick and tired of being sick and tired of clobbering myself with my own two-by-four ego.

The principle of the Tenth Step was the key for me: whenever *I* was wrong to promptly admit it. I began making amends to my wife. Each time we'd have an argument or there was emotional pain, I'd get away somewhere and do a short written inventory on it. (I began to believe what it says in the *Twelve and Twelve* that whenever I'm disturbed, there's something wrong with *me*.) What was I feeling? Why? Where was *I* wrong? Then, trying not to remind her of her wrong, I'd confess my own and walk away. Often I'd have to say it in a note because I was afraid I'd open my big ego and hurt her again. I was beginning to conceal the glorious story of how right I was and to confess where I was wrong.

It worked. *I* felt better. I started making similar amends to the boy. "I was wrong for rejecting you when I chewed you out about that misplaced tool." I got good feelings inside whenever I did this. I got stronger. I sinned against them less often. The key to my joy was seeing, admitting, and correcting the way I related to others.

I had made those "big" grand amends as soon as I had come on the program. Such as, "I'm sorry for all the wrong I did to you. . . ." And all that good stuff. But that never *changed* anything. I had *always* said I'M SORRY. It was the little specific daily amends that started making the big difference.

I fixed the damage to the back door. I enjoyed it.

I discovered I liked fixing things. I liked fixing me. And I liked fixing the marriage. (I had always been the one who wanted to be fixed.) But I had to stop trying to fix *her*. I began taking an interest in what she was interested in: the house, her stained glass, my responsibility as a provider.

All the while, I kept coming more and more off lust and my other spiritual drugs: resentment-anger-hostility, fear, dependency, judging others, people-pleasing, self-glorification. They all began to yield *once I could start seeing and accepting what I really was (my defects) and taking God's action on it.*

After four or five years in sobriety, the difference in the marriage and family relationships was markedly better; the breakthrough had been made. Thank God, and thanks to the patience, love, and understanding of the wife and children (the older ones had long been gone from the home). I knew it, and they knew it. No matter what happened, things would never be the same. (And as with sobriety, we still have a marriage only one day at a time.) We had crossed the threshold into a new beginning.

Throughout this time I was progressively getting rid of all the old "bottles" I had stashed away in the cupboards of my heart. Those invisible attachments to whom I knew I could always turn if I ever decided to take the "out" of last resort and walk out on the marriage. I hadn't been acting on them, but they were in there, just in case. . . . Had I been able to see what these still meant to me and discard them sooner, things would have gotten better sooner. Somewhere along the line, I came to a commitment of permanency with my wife. In my heart. It meant giving up the right to run to anyone else, ever—one day at a time.

Instead of those dismal Sunday morning talks, we were starting to talk and touch as friends. I had just begun to glimpse my wife as an individual, had begun to see the limitless depth of what was in there—a person, unique, vulnerable, human. God was there.

During periods of voluntary sexual abstinence we

came to realize that true union could not be based on sex or dependency, of whatever sort. During those times we discovered we were actually closer together, on a deeper level. She discovered she didn't have to give herself sexually to earn her husband's favor, and I discovered that I was drawn to her as a person and actually preferred the warmth of nonsexual relating insofar as the fostering of our union was concerned.

We still have rough times, and I'm sure there'll be more, with more pain and desperation, but things are getting better and are the best ever. Paradoxically, we still have a marriage only one day at a time. Release. We give each other the right to fail. Turns out neither of us had any idea of what marriage had to offer. Words can never tell. It's like knowing my God personally; words can never tell. I feel we're just now at the very beginning—the right beginning.

Conclusions:

- The physical and emotional state of my wife, children, cats, and doorways have been the truest indicators of the real me.
- Sober is not well.
- It takes years of sobriety, pain, and hard work to even begin to heal a marriage.
- Healing in the family begins by staying sober, going to meetings, and working the Steps. It continues by staying sober, going to meetings, and working the Steps. It can end by not staying sober, not going to meetings, and not working the Steps.
- My own diseased attitudes and actions kept me looking at others negatively so I wouldn't have to see and bear my own wrongfulness.
- My spouse, children, other family and program members, friends, and coworkers are part of my healing and recovery when I allow that to happen.
- Marriage is a sanctifying force both in our lives and the children's as well. And that's why for me the rela-

tionships didn't do it and fell short. They were rooted either in lust or unhealthy dependency. They were open-ended; there was always that "out"; we were cheated of having to stick with it and walk through to victory, beauty, and song. And God was not there.

- My spouse and children: They are God's gift, through all the pain, to the completion of myself as a person and member of the human family.
- My own attitude and recovery are the key. They open the door to recovery and spiritual life in my family and larger circle of relationships.

Overcoming Lust and Temptation

When we withdraw from our habits and are able to stay sexually sober for some length of time, we discover that even though we may not be acting out our compulsion, the obsession is still with us, though it may seem to disappear for a time. Lust, as we have seen, assumes many disguises, which we begin to recognize in sobriety as time goes on. For one person, lust may be lusting after someone. For another, it may be the obsession to be lusted after. For yet another, lust may appear as a desperate sexual or emotional need for someone. In any case, it is the inner disposition of the heart that is the real problem, and the work of recovery continues with altered attitudes and gaining progressive victory over lust.

Lust only yields to the slow, patient working of the program in the context of others who are doing the same. This is one reason we need the fellowship of sobriety on a continuing basis. The rewards are unending, giving us the true freedom we always wanted.

In the following piece, a member tells how he overcame his obsession with lust. For many, these suggestions have proven to be useful in maintaining sobriety and overcoming lust and temptation.

How I Overcame My Obsession with Lust

How did I do it? I didn't. A woman in AA told me after she spoke in a meeting, quoting Chapter 5 in *Alcoholics Anonymous*, that "God could and would, if He were sought." And that's how I did it. By letting God do it. Because I couldn't. But God could and would—and did. But I had to go to meetings to learn things like that. "Meetings, meetings, meetings, meetings, meetings . . ." That's what they told me. "Just keep bringing the body." "Work the Steps, work the Steps, work the Steps, work the Steps, work the Steps." Going to meetings and working the Steps; that's how I did it. That's how I learned to let "the grace of God enter to expel the obsession." Here's what worked for me:

1. Stop practicing the compulsion. I stopped acting out sexually in any and all forms, including sex with myself and nonmarital relationships. There could be no relief from the obsession of lust while still practicing the acts of lust.

2. Stop feeding the obsession. This meant eliminating from what was under my control all printed and visual materials and other symbols of my tyranny. I had to stop feeding my lust by looking around, in my use of television, movies, and music; and by using and listening to the language of lust.

I also had to stop living only and always inside my own head. That's one of the great fringe benefits of going to a lot of meetings. Most of us sexaholics really live on the inside of our heads; we're seldom in the real world.

3. Participate in the fellowship of the program. I don't know of anyone who can stay sober and free of the obsession of lust without such fellowship. I couldn't. *Fellowship* is where the action is, where the magic is, where Connection is, where feeling *part of* is.

At first, all I could do was *attend* meetings. Then I followed the suggestion of getting involved in the mechanics of meetings: setting up, cleaning up, holding jobs such as literature chairman, treasurer, or secretary. Getting involved made me feel I could be *part of*, instead of *apart from*—my old nemesis. Later, I would be able to go out for coffee, start meeting with others one-on-one, and begin the painful but necessary process of growing up by coming out.

4. Admit powerlessness. At the very beginning, all I could do when the compulsion struck was cry out, "I'm powerless; please help me!" Sometimes a hundred times a day. Powerlessness was the most beautiful word in the world to me then as I was coming to experience the First Step at depth. It still is. Later I would discover that I was really powerless over *me*.

The more I had fought lust before, the more it fought back; all my willpower seemed to empower lust rather than hold it in check. Reading Step One in the *Twelve and Twelve* helped me see that my powerlessness was the "firm bedrock upon which happy and purposeful lives may be built" (p. 21). I finally stopped trying to stop. Only by admitting lust's power over me to others in the fellowship could I receive power over my lust.

5. Surrender. Without surrender, mere admission of powerlessness fails to connect us with our Higher Power. At first for me it was surrender to the group where I began attending meetings. This was simply going to the meetings and being as honest, open-minded, and willing as I could. This was how I came to experience the Second Step and have hope that a Power greater than myself could restore me to sanity. This was what prepared the way for the Third Step surrender later on, when it would be to God as I understood Him.

As far as my lust was concerned, I knew exactly what surrender meant and what I had to do. Every time I was tempted from within or without I would say, "I surrender the right to lust after this person; please take it away." And like it says, "God could and would . . ." and did. I may have had some discomfort or fear and may have had to repeat the surrender over and over again, but it worked. It felt scary at first, but I was staying sober, and it was slowly getting easier, one temptation at a time.

6. Bring the inside out. As I began to see that I would apparently never be cured of the possibility of lusting, I had to bring other Steps to bear on me. Steps Four and Five opened the door to being able to look at myself critically. This was probably the most important change of attitude in my early recovery.

But with lust, I had to keep taking mini-inventories, as suggested in the Fifth and Tenth Steps. Whenever I felt some experience, image, memory, or thought was controlling me, as was often the case, I would bring it to the light, talking it out with another program person. Get the air and sunlight on it. Lust hates the light and flees from it; it loves the dark secret recesses of my being. And once I let it lodge there, it's like a fungus and starts flourishing—the athlete's foot of the soul. But as soon as I bring it to the light, exposing it to another recovering sexaholic, the power it has over me is broken. Light kills lust. I did this with specific experiences, not in generalities. Sometimes it meant imposing on a person's time, but it cleaned me out and kept me sober. Every time I talked it out in surrender, the power of that memory or experience was broken. Another new and powerful breakthrough.

7. Trust. As I was able more and more to live above my lust, learning to trust more and more in God's power to expel the obsession, I soon learned to begin each day with a prayer of putting myself and my lust in God's hands, just for that day. This meant I was learning to live without lust and really *wanted* to be free of it.

Now I begin each day with the Third Step prayer (from *Alcoholics Anonymous*, p. 63), changing the wording to suit my own case. It usually goes something like this:

> Please keep me sober from my lust today, because I can't. . . . I offer you my will and life today to do and build with as you will. Relieve me of the bondage of self today that I may better do your will. Take away my difficulties today, that victory over them may bear witness to those I would help of your great power, love, and way of life. Give me what I need today. Thy will, not mine, be done today.

8. Use the literature of the program. The *Twelve and Twelve* and *Alcoholics Anonymous* were my first guides in working the Steps. Again and again I found what I needed in those original documents that launched the Twelve Step program. Many of us now find that working the principles outlined in our SA literature adds another dimension and is very helpful. Using it in the solitude and privacy of our own quiet times, we gain insights about ourselves and our recovery in a way uniquely suited to who and where we are.

9. Go to work on the other defects. I discovered to my utter amazement that lust was not my root problem at all; it was just another symptom of my underlying spiritual illness—diseased attitudes. Lust was just one more manifestation of this huge negative force within me that had to bust out any way it could. As soon as lust started to go, resentment started taking its place. Then fear. Then a judging spirit. It was like trying to stop a leak in a dam. While you're trying to plug up one hole, it springs a leak somewhere else, because there's this huge body of water behind the dam, and its pressure is going to make it break out at the weakest spot.

This huge body of water, it turns out, is the destructive negative side of me. And the degree to which I can connect into the positive Power (God) is the degree to which I disconnect from the negative in all its forms. Thank God, today I have a choice.

The fringe benefit of *having* to work on my defects to rid myself of the obsession of lust is finally being able to plug into Life. But I can't be free of any obsession while I'm drunk on another. I can't be free of lust while drunk on resentment. And so on. . . .

I went to Step Study meetings to learn how others were actually getting victory over their defects. I was told that one of the best ways to nip a resentful thought in the bud is to pray for the person I resented. Ask for them what you want for yourself, they suggested. It worked! My first employer in sobriety was the object of scores of such prayers daily. They didn't seem to do him much good (who knows?), but they kept me from falling into the snake pit of resentment.

10. Learn to give instead of take. This technique worked on lust too. Whenever I'd catch a likely image in the corner of my eye, instead of obeying the impulse to look and drink, I'd keep looking straight ahead while praying for that person. It might be a simple, "God bless her and give her what she needs." Or, depending on the intensity of the lust stimulus, it might be more fervent: "God bless her and make her a blessing; Thy will be done in her life."

I began doing the same for models in ads that had a similar power over me. Whenever I do this kind of thing, I feel good; I get something back that is clean and strong and free and good. I somehow become a channel for releasing good into me instead of opening up a conduit of lust for evil to come in. The measure I drink in of that image is the measure I am enslaved by it; the measure I *give* out to another is the measure I am released from its power. Plus, it's so much easier to give than try that old self-mortification kind of willpower.

Try it sometime: You cannot lust after the one you're praying for in such a manner. Here's an experience related by a woman member:

> *"I remember early in sobriety seeing a very suggestive video in a department store. I got drawn into it, and before I knew what hit me, that image took me over! So I started praying for that singer, over and over. And it worked! I have tried this many times since, and it always works for me."*

This action may also serve to make indirect amends to all the anonymous objects of my lust and sex acts—those many strangers I have helped confirm in their destructive way of life. It seems to be a law of the universe: The measure I give is the measure I get back.

11. Get an SA sponsor. I needed someone who could see me better than I could, even though he might have had some problems of his own. (Everyone I used as a sponsor had imperfections big enough to turn me away if I wanted such an excuse.) It was my reaching out and taking direction that worked. I made regular contact and followed directions. It helped make me teachable and saved me a lot of grief and lost time.

12. **Make friends in the program.** My sexaholism had forced me away from true intimacy. I had become a loner and a love cripple. To recover, I had to begin coming out of isolation and connect with people. But I didn't know how. At first, I was forced to make phone calls to stay sober. Then, as I shared with others in my distress and they shared their trials with me, a common bond developed. Partners in sobriety—what a boon! It helped change that lonely grey inner world of the separated self into the bright sunlight of glad times shared together. Victory over lust was not the grim experience I had feared. I was getting connected to life and began to feel impulses of joy. I was beginning to have what my lust had really been looking for. I can't have the inner freedom from the need to lust without this real connection.

13. **Carry the message of your recovery.** At first, I began by guardedly talking about my sexual obsession and desire for recovery to those who gave hints of similar problems. I didn't know this was part of working the Twelfth Step; I was doing it because I wanted to. Then I started sharing the truth of my experience *in* other meetings I was going to. Very few ever responded, but the point is, it was helping *me*.

Bill W. of AA used to say that Twelfth Step work "takes a little money and a lot of time." And I found that being willing to spend a fraction of the time and money on carrying the message of my recovery that I had spent on my habit helped keep me sober. When I give freely of my time and means in this manner, I get back the priceless gifts of freedom from lust plus joy and serenity. In the process, I have also taken the first faltering steps at learning how to love another human being. I couldn't ask for a bigger payoff.

14. Practice taking the actions of love. Negative sobriety—simply not doing it—fizzles out after a while. That's all I had for many months, and that's why one day, with no particular problems and having just told my old high school friend I was a *recovered* sex drunk, I proceeded to "go back out there." I didn't know what hit me. I didn't slip; I fell!

The crucial thing about my recovery is that unless I find what my lust is really looking for, I'm not going to make it. Stopping the negatives without connecting with the positive is no good. For the sexaholic like me it's all or nothing. "Half measures availed us nothing," *Alcoholics Anonymous* says on page 59. And so it is with me.

Program people taught me that right thinking never produced right actions, but if I took the right actions, the right thinking and feelings followed. I discovered in sexual sobriety that I was not inclined to touch my wife except when it was a sensual, erotic, or sexual thing. I never touched her simply as a *person*, a *spiritual* touch, if you will. But I learned that if I took the action of touching her as a person, the feeling of wanting to followed. I'll never forget the first time in sobriety when, after that awful separation and chaos, one day I was able to glance into her eyes and reach out and touch her arm and say "Thank you." How the power of love flowed through that connection! *After* I took the action. It brought tears to my eyes.

Another time, my wife had fixed supper, but my negative emotions had taken control again and I was on my way out the door—to nowhere. I managed to stop long enough to call my sponsor, who gruffly reminded me that it was Sunday and he was busy (none of my sponsors pretended to be saints). In ten seconds he saw through the "problem" (self-obsession) and said, "Sit down and eat your supper" and hung up. I mechanically sat down and ate the supper she had prepared for me. And that awful feeling of having to run passed. I took the action, and the feeling followed.

The greatest opportunity for practicing love is not in meetings but in my own household. And that's the very place it's hardest to do. It's actually easier for me to pray for prostitutes and other SA members than take the actions of love toward my wife and children. But I have to do it or I can't break through into life. And I want to live!

Another action of love that seems to produce remarkable results is praying for my wife; again, asking for her the very best that I want for myself. This goes along with one of the above items on practicing giving instead of taking. Since I had shut myself up to my spouse as the only sexual expression, I discovered, in taking my own inventory, that my dependency on her was unhealthy. As a result, I abstained sexually over a considerable period of time, with her consent, so I could deal with my dependency.

Afterward, I concluded that I was willing to go without sex completely as long as my dependency was still infected with any aspect of "buying and selling." "Wife or no wife, we simply do not stop drinking so long as we place dependence upon other people ahead of dependence on God." (*Alcoholics Anonymous*, p. 98)

Thus, every time I had a negative feeling about my wife, I prayed for her. I didn't feel like doing it, but I did. It works. But I have to be willing to give up the resentment and forgive. That's where Steps Six and Seven come in.

15. Recognize and feed your hunger for God. As I came into another stage of awareness, I began to sense that my most basic drive was neither sex nor power nor whatever but my spiritual hunger—my God-drive, the need for God himself. It seems what I'm really looking for in these visual drinking bouts with lust as I walk down the glamorous avenues of the world is a Connection. What I really want is to make the Big C with the Source of my life. And in my illness, Woman is the source of my being, my god. Lust deceives me into believing *that* is what I cannot live without, when it is really God I cannot live without.

Thus, another technique I use successfully in the moment of temptation is to ask—*before* turning the head and drinking—"Whatever it is I'm really looking for now, let me please find it in You." Again and again and again, with every person I'm attracted to, the prayer goes up. It works for me. And what better way to take the Eleventh Step?

This principle of displacement works for all my negative emotions. I fill the place that lust or resentment or fear or judging another would take in my mind with the presence of God. Substitute the Real for the unreal. I reach out for God in that situation. It helps to close my eyes while doing this.

16. Cast it out. There are certain times when I've felt like I was walking through a lust minefield, with charges going off all around me. It was so unusually severe and persistent, that I've wondered if I were under some kind of attack. At such times I have taken the extreme measure of casting it out vocally as though it were a foreign evil presence. Not in my own power or authority, but in the power and authority of my Higher Power. I don't claim to understand this, and I don't make a big deal about it, but it has worked for me when I seemed otherwise totally at the mercy of what was going on. In ensuing years, I've heard other members share similar experiences.

17. Take refuge in God. Often I call on God's presence as a shield to protect me from my own lust or emotions or from the lust or emotions of others. Again, as soon as I feel overwhelmed or see the image in the corner of my eye and want to turn and drink, I'll say, "I take Your presence to shield me from my lust (or whatever it is)." But *I* have to take up that shield! I have to turn to Him for refuge.

Another telegram for help I send up today, after some years of sobriety, is something like this: "I don't want any part of this lust (or other negative emotion or attitude); I want You to take it." It works every time. But *I* have to give it away.

18. Look lust in the eye. Now I'm also discovering a new way of dealing with the day's temptations so they won't come back and hit me in my dreams. I've noticed that instead of true surrender, I can sometimes, during the day, push lust down out of sight by sheer willpower. There have been times after doing this when lust has later resurfaced in erotic dreams in such a way that I knew I could act out sexually in my sleep without even touching myself and knowing I had the choice! How *super*-powerful those temptations are! And scary! They get your attention.

I've had enough of those close calls to take preventive action. Just before going to sleep, I deliberately recall to my mind's eye each lust temptation that stuck with me during the day, looking that person full in the face. I bring each person to the light, before God, as I surrender, admitting my powerlessness over lust. I say, "*You* know my heart, how I really want to lust. I send it away to You. Come be victorious over my lust; I don't want any of it—conscious or subconscious. I want *You* to bear it for me. Please keep me sober from *all* my lust tonight." Often I'll add a prayer for that person involved in my temptation, going outward in giving. It's my way of staying clean at the subconscious level. It's also my way of coping with fear of falling in my sleep.

Summary

These various ways of overcoming lust take practice, but they work. It took many years to program myself to lusting as I did; I found it takes time to stop that and program myself to reality.

Whenever I began any of the above techniques, it felt artificial and forced. I didn't *want* to do it; it didn't feel right. I try not to trust those diseased feelings any more; they're what got me here.

Taking some of these measures was like killing off part of me, they were so much against my natural inclinations. But I found that what I needed to be set free was to take such forceful stands against my old ways of thinking and doing. These were breakthroughs into right action.

I always have to remember that it's not the person out there that's causing my lust and discomfort; it's *me.* This brings up one final point. The lust I want to stay sober from is *my* lust. I made it what it is. I *am* a lustaholic. In the same way, I *am* a resentful and angry person, a judging and condemning person, a fearful person. There is no healing for me if I deny, evade, or cover my defects. "I'm as sick as my secrets."

On the other hand, I can live free of the power any and all these defects have over me by resorting to God instead of such negative emotions. I thus have a daily, hourly reprieve from my lust, etc., based on maintaining the right attitude. And I maintain the right attitude by working the Steps and Traditions and going to meetings, meetings, meetings, meetings, meetings.

God has apparently not chosen to eradicate my defective self so that I am no longer capable of lust, resentment, fear, and the rest. If he ever did that, I'd have no need of Him; I'd be an automaton. It's progressive victory *over* my defects that's the name of the game. I myself am what could be called a "sinner." But I take from God the power I do not have in myself to transcend my sins. *Victory through powerlessness by the grace of God!*

That's the beautiful paradox of this program: In and through my powerlessness, I receive the power—and love—that come from above.

And that's the difference between self-denial and surrender. Self-denial—white-knuckling it—brought misery and failure. Acknowledging what I am, surrendering, and relying on God's power bring release, freedom, and joy.

Recovery is an inside job.

The above list of suggestions on overcoming lust will be forever incomplete, as will the experiences reflected in this book. Everyone who stays sober and grows in recovery will add to our collective experience what works for them. Our lives, such as they are, are the real book, "known and read of all men." As time goes by, more is revealed, and it keeps getting better. This is the great adventure of recovery from sexaholism.

A Vision for You

We realize we know only a little. God will constantly disclose more to you and to us. Ask Him in your morning meditation what you can do each day for the man who is still sick. The answers will come, if your own house is in order. But obviously you cannot transmit something you haven't got. See to it that your relationship with Him is right, and great events will come to pass for you and countless others. This is the Great Fact for us.

Abandon yourself to God as you understand God. Admit your faults to Him and to your fellows. Clear away the wreckage of your past. Give freely of what you find and join us. We shall be with you in the Fellowship of the Spirit, and you will surely meet some of us as you trudge the Road of Happy Destiny.

May God bless you and keep you—until then.

(*Alcoholics Anonymous*, p. 164)

Sexaholics Anonymous will be glad to hear from you.
Address P. O. Box 111910, Nashville, TN 37222-1910.

PART III

Starting a New SA Group
Meetings—How They Work
The Sobriety Definition

The Fellowship of Sobriety

To have a share in any earthly inheritance is to diminish the share of the other inheritors. In the inheritance of the [Fellowship], that which each has goes to increase the possession of the rest.

. . .

In this inheritance, a man may desire and endeavor to obtain his share without selfish prejudice to others; nay, to fail of our share in it, would be to deprive others of a portion of theirs.

. . .

The true share . . . is not what you have to keep, but what you have to give away.

. . .

Every one of us is something that the other is not and therefore knows something—it may be without knowing that he knows it—which no one else knows. It is every one's business . . . as inheritor in it all, to give his portion to the rest; for we are one family, with God at the head and heart of it. . .

George MacDonald, 1891

Starting a New SA Group

*The Group**

General

The primary purpose of an SA group is "to carry its message to the sexaholic who still suffers" (Tradition 5). Traditionally, as with AA, any two or more sexaholics meeting for purposes of sexual sobriety by following the SA program may consider themselves an SA group, provided that as a group they have no affiliation with any outside enterprise or other fellowship and receive no outside support. The following are suggestions gained from our experience to date.

Starting the Group

1. Find a weekly meeting place and set the time. At first, this may be a private home or office, where anonymity

---

*The following material is taken from the SA *Meeting Guide*. Answers to many of the questions and issues often confronting new or established SA groups are suggested in this material. All members are urged to read what has proven to be of value in maintaining successful groups and good meeting quality.

and privacy can be assured. Churches are often willing to provide facilities. Check with churches and other organizations where other Twelve Step program meetings are held. Often such facilities are made available to other groups. Check with the SA Central Office.
2. Select a group secretary, treasurer, and literature chairperson. These are explained below. Members who accept these responsibilities serve the group; they do not govern, in accordance with Tradition Two.
3. Advise the SA Central Office of the name and phone number of the secretary and an alternate contact and meeting particulars. Each SA group should have at least one contact and one backup contact for the SA Central Office for referrals. Advise Central Office of changes.

Secretary

Should have successful sexual sobriety; length of that sobriety should be agreed upon by the group conscience. Suggested term of office is six months or a year, although each group is autonomous and may hold elections whenever it wishes. Rotating leadership is best. Secretary's responsibilities include:

1. Selects a person or sees to it that a person is there to lead each meeting and provides that person with meeting format and literature. A good idea is to select the leader a week in advance.
2. Is responsible for the meeting place and notifying members.
3. Maintains communications with SA Central Office and notifies it of any changes.
4. Maintains communication with other nearby SA groups and SA as a whole. Announces SA conventions and get-togethers.
5. Sees to it that the *Essay* newsletter is available to all members. Each member may also ask to be placed on the *Essay* mailing list.

6. Handles necessary correspondence and phone calls or delegates these.
7. Calls business or group-conscience meetings.
8. Seeks to incorporate the principles of our Twelve Traditions into the spirit and activities of the group.

Treasurer

Should have successful sobriety; length of that sobriety should be agreed upon by the group conscience. Same term of office as secretary. Responsibilities include:

1. Is custodian and disburser of money received by passing the basket at meetings. Collections are usually counted and recorded by the treasurer and one other member.
2. Keeps detailed accounts of group's finances and reports on this at business meetings.
3. When directed by the group, sends regular group contribution to SA Central Office for national and world services. The fellowship has evolved a means of supporting its world services that is working. Individual groups, either at every meeting or on a regular basis, pass the basket around a second time, the proceeds of which go entirely to support the SA Central Office. Some groups have the policy that a certain percentage of excess money left over after paying all group expenses be sent regularly to the Central Office. All groups are urged to develop some means of contributing a share in our expanding worldwide Twelfth Step work. Such contributions support the work of the Central Office. SA is totally self-supporting.
4. All member contributions to Sexaholics Anonymous are tax-deductible, since SA is a nonprofit, exempt organization as registered with the U.S. Internal Revenue Service. For countries other than U.S.A., check appropriate ordinances.

Literature Chairperson

Orders literature from the SA Central Office and from A.A. Sees to it that meetings always have a supply of *Sexaholics Anonymous*, the SA brochure, *Recovery Continues*, and whatever other SA literature is available, such as *Essay* and *Discovering the Principles*. AA literature is the only non-SA material used in meetings. (See the article "Meeting Quality and Use of Non-SA Literature" in *Discovering the Principles.)*

Steering Committee

This is a means for handling the group or intergroup business and policy matters in groups large enough to have one. Service on this committee, like most SA responsibilities, is on a rotating basis. All of the group officers are usually included on the steering committee, with as many other members added as needed. The steering committee serves the group or groups by providing a convenient experienced cross-section of sober group membership to take care of group(s) functioning.

Other Positions

Some groups may find it convenient to have refreshment, setup, and cleanup committees. Some groups operate well with only a secretary and treasurer. The members of the group decide the service structure it needs.

The Meetings

Closed Meetings

As a general principle, it is suggested that SA meetings be open only to those who want to stop their sexually self-destructive thinking and behavior. "The only requirement for membership is a desire to stop lusting and become sexually sober" (Tradition Three). There are hundreds of thousands of people with sexual and marital problems of every conceivable description. Many may want a support group, but not sexual sobriety, and some may be more intent on changing SA than changing themselves. Keeping meetings "closed" (open to sexaholics only) will help protect the membership from the curious and the insincere. At the same time, we realize that desire for sobriety can be hidden among mixed motives and may grow in time and with participation in the fellowship.

General Meeting Format

Suggested meeting formats are included with this guide. Length of meetings is usually an hour and one-half. Meetings should begin promptly. Being responsible in this regard helps our recovery. We're acting for the good of the whole, which turns out to be the best for us as individuals.

Types of Meetings

- Participation meetings that allow opportunity for all members to share.
- Step- or book-study meetings using the SA book and the *Twelve and Twelve*. Portions are read and then discussed by members in terms of their own sobriety (or lack of it) and needs. Seeing how this is done in other Twelve Step program book-study or Step-study meetings can be very helpful to SA groups with no prior experience. One of the best things we can do is have meetings where we read the SA book together.
- Speaker meetings. After the standard preliminaries, one, two, or three sober SA members tell their stories, following the traditional outline of What It Was Like, What Happened, and What It's Like Now. Speakers are only those who are sexaholics in SA and who have achieved a considerable period of sexual sobriety. Use of notes or prepared speeches is discouraged. Experience has shown that it is better to speak from the heart from wherever we are at that time. We don't *tell*; we *share*. We can only bear witness to the truth of our

own experience. We do not have nonsexaholics speak in SA meetings.
- Combination speaker and participation meetings.

Mixed Meetings

In new groups, the question sometimes arises as to whether meetings should be mixed, with both women and men. Less frequently, questions arise about mixing those from different lifestyles or mixing singles and marrieds. It is understandable that some of us experience initial discomfort at attending mixed meetings; sexaholism is the *mis*connection with other bodies and spirits. For some, the objects of our lust or resentment are sitting right there next to us, and we can imbibe and get drunk without so much as batting an eyelash! (That's why we avoid inappropriate attire in meetings, out of consideration for others.)

What we tend to forget is that our drug is not really "out there" in another person, but within our own hearts and minds. It is this fact that makes our program so all-encompassing, regardless of whether we're in a meeting, outside on the street, or in a closet praying. Our problem is lust, misplaced dependency, and defective attitudes. What better place to work on overcoming temptation than the sanctuary of a meeting where temptations may be present? This is where we can bring temptation to the light, talk about it, and work through it *without* having to lust, sexualize, or go into dependency, anger, or rebellion. The meeting is the crucible in which our recovery can be safely tested and purified.

Considering what we are, reason might seem to indicate that we segregate to "protect" ourselves or so that we might have greater freedom "expressing our unique problems and concerns." We have found the very opposite to be true: In the long run, it has proven better for us to be together. The only exception to this seems to be with those who have not surrendered lust and are still acting out in some manner. Having such persons present in meetings where they make sexual or other improper moves on members is a threat to individual recovery and group unity. If such cases arise—and there have been very few—the group should discuss the matter in a business meeting and deal with it at the group conscience level. The group learns from such experiences.

We benefit from seeing reflections of the problem and recovery from other points of view. For example, after the initial fear of having a woman member come into an all-male group, men typically have testified to its value, saying they would not have it otherwise. Likewise, when women work through their fear of such a situation, they too recognize the value of meeting together. We all have the same problem. When we disclose the thoughts and intents of our hearts in surrender, we identify with one another at depth. Our common problem is not sexual at all; it is spiritual. We identify at the level of feelings: guilt, shame, remorse, loneliness, resentment, anger, rage, fear. . . . On the other hand, we are careful not to be a temptation to others in the *way* we talk about our sexual acting-out. As susceptible as we are to suggestion, our lust can get carried away into realms never before imagined. This is why we can quietly raise our hands if descriptions are getting too graphic or suggestive. The meeting should not be a place where our lust horizons are being broadened.

After any initial discomfort from mixed meetings, members come to see their benefit. Most people come into SA to *stop* lusting and become sexually sober. When we are united by this common commitment to sobriety and recovery, any uneasiness that may arise can be worked out. Such a process seems to be a necessary part of our recovery, freedom, and growth.

Twelfth Step Attraction

The impulse of life arising out of our Twelfth Step reality carries the message of our recovery to other sexaholics. Contacts are made in our own personal lives where we live and work in the world. The Central Office can often supply names of serious inquirers in any given area. These are ready-made contacts, waiting for that precious person-to-person encounter to introduce them to sexual sobriety. The Central Office also can make available to groups the experiences of other groups that have gone through similar problems and issues. (Read the article "Publicity and the Twelfth Step," in *Discovering the Principles.*)

How Do We Deal with Newcomers?

Many groups use the following approach: Before inquirers attend their first meeting, one or more sober SA members talk with them on the phone or, preferably, meet with them. If the inquirer is a woman, there should be a woman SA member present, and if a man, there should be a male member present. Telling them our story usually encourages them to tell their own; and once newcomers do this, they (and we) are better able to tell whether they identify and want recovery. *By all means, give newcomers a copy of the SA brochure and tell them your story.*

Depending on the situation, we may feel it appropriate to ask certain questions: (a) "What brings you to SA?" (b) "What do you want from SA?" (c) "Do you want sexual sobriety?" (We don't hesitate to read from the sections in this book titled "What Is a Sexaholic and What Is Sexual Sobriety?" and "The Sobriety Definition.") (d) "What do you want to *stop*?" (e) "Are you here for any reasons other than your own personal recovery?" Some have had occasion to ask whether the person was connected with the media in any way.

Our common experience indicates that people who are opposed to our concept of sexual sobriety can cause division and other problems. We recognize, however, that the desire for sobriety can grow and work in stages, one level at a time. Let's deal with newcomers as we would want to be dealt with if we were in their shoes. The best way to introduce SA to a newcomer is to tell our own story: what it was like, what happened, and what it's like now. In other words, we're saying, "This is what we're about; is this for you?" (Read the article "What Can We Say to Newcomers in Relationships?" in *Discovering the Principles.*)

Precautions

1. We suggest that no ads of any kind be placed in newspapers, periodicals, on bulletin boards, etc., even in other Twelve Step meetings, that disclose the whereabouts of SA meetings. Advertising time and place of meetings to the general public can cause problems. For the same reason we suggest that no signs be put up outside meeting places identifying them as SA meetings.
2. In certain situations it is advisable that only SA members know when and where SA meetings are being held. This may include those agencies and institutions that want to put us on their referral lists. We can give them a P.O. box number or phone numbers of SA members available as contacts. As time goes on, these situations may change so that less caution is needed.
3. We suggest that before seeking or consenting to media interviews or coverage, members contact the Central Office. Our national policy is that individuals and groups do not grant interviews. *In today's instant-media climate, this can affect other SA groups and/or SA as a whole.* (See Tradition Four.) Once an article appears in the press, it becomes common property of the media. Thus, an article in some local newspaper may wind up getting onto one of the national wire services, and if it happens to mention our address, we can be inundated with thousands of inquiries with no means to handle them. At present we feel it wiser to grow from the inside out, rather than from the outside in. *Please contact the SA Central Office of questions regarding the media arise.* (Read the article "Publicity and the Twelfth Step," in *Discovering the Principles.*)
4. Before a group lists a telephone number in the name of Sexaholics Anonymous, it should be carefully con-

sidered by the entire group and neighboring groups. Such a listing can imply existence of an office and staff. It is not a step to be taken lightly, even if no address is given. Once it is done, there must be those who will always be available to answer and carry out the responsibilities that ensue. In that act you are offering a *public* service; you become subject to the public. On the other hand, having such a phone listing is one of the best points of contact with other sexaholics seeking help.

5. We suggest limiting smoking to outside the meeting area proper. Increasing numbers of people are not smoking, and some members have medical problems related to cigarette smoke. Increasing numbers of other groups are practicing this approach as awareness increases. Each SA group is autonomous and must consider this problem for itself. However, if this precedent can be accepted from the very beginning, as it has been for most SA groups, the question need never become an issue.

Group Conscience Meetings

Group officers or individual members can call for group conscience (business) meetings to decide on all matters pertaining to the group: election of officers, terms of office, length of sobriety required for holding office and voting, finances, and other matters affecting the group and its relation to other groups and SA as a whole.

The group conscience determines the length of sexual sobriety required before a member can vote in the meeting. (Read the articles "Group Conscience Meetings and the Twelve Traditions" and "What's a Group Conscience?" in *Discovering the Principles*.)

SA Get-Togethers

The Sexaholics Anonymous fellowship has an increasing number of regional, national, and international get-togethers, lasting from one day to entire weekends. These are sponsored by local groups or areas and announced in the *Essay* newsletter. These have proven to be unforgettable experiences. Here we meet and enjoy friends old and new. We rediscover laughter and have fun together. Our recovery is validated and enhanced in new and stronger ways. We see how SA is working in different groups and at the national and international levels. Local and personal problems come to take on a different cast when viewed against the backdrop of the larger experience. We come away strengthened. We have a new sense of purpose, understanding ourselves and others better, and having an increased bond of love, unity, and joy. And we sense as never before the loving care and direction of the One guiding and watching over us all.

SA Is Self-Supporting

Sexaholics Anonymous is entirely self-supporting at the group, national, and international levels. We accept no money or gratuities from persons or organizations outside SA. Being responsible for our own finances is part of being responsible for our own recovery. This time-tested Seventh Tradition has served us well: *"Every SA group ought to be fully self-supporting, declining outside contributions."* Member and group contributions make up the bulk of support for the Central Office world services, with some additional funds accruing from literature sales.

The fellowship has evolved a means of supporting its world services that is working. Individual groups, either at every meeting or on a regular basis, pass the basket around a second time, the proceeds of which go entirely to support the SA Central Office. Some groups have the policy that a certain percentage of excess money left over after paying all group expenses be sent regularly to the Central Office. *All groups are urged to develop some means of contributing a share in our expanding worldwide Twelfth Step work.* The Central Office, increasingly well-equipped to handle the growing volume of mail and telephone inquiries, employs help for secretarial and other services in commercial offices in Nashville, Tennessee.

Financial statements are provided in the *Essay* newsletter and are also available on request.

All member contributions to Sexaholics Anonymous are tax-deductible, since SA is a nonprofit, exempt organization as registered with the U.S. Internal Revenue Service. For countries other than the U.S.A., check appropriate ordinances.

Meetings—How They Work

"As I come into the fellowship, I'm confronted with my disease. First, in my initial contacts with other members; then in meeting after meeting. But there are parts of the disease still hidden in that deep hole inside me, sides of me I never want you to see, and eventually they start festering. So, one by one, I'm forced to get rid of them. The problem is, how do I keep my disease from always running into a dark corner?"

That's how one member put it in trying to describe something of what happens in meetings. The problem is our blind sides; we all have them. So, the question for us is, How do we work our personal programs and conduct our meetings and fellowship so as to "walk in the light"? Here's what has been working for us:

1. By getting sober and staying sober and holding to the concept of sexual sobriety in our SA meetings. Without sobriety we have nothing to offer anyone. SA offers sexual sobriety, progressive victory over lust, and recovery. When this is our aim, meetings can become a sanctuary of serenity and light.

2. By not imposing uniformity. We don't prescribe doing the Steps by formula or in exactly the same way some other member does them. We do the Steps in our own way and time; we "Live and Let Live." But working the Steps *does* work for us.
3. By telling the side of our stories we really don't want to tell. This is different than a mere "sexalog," relating our sexual experiences. It is rigorous self-searching and self-revealing honesty about every aspect of our lives. We are fitting the pieces of our lives together differently every time we tell our stories or share.
4. By telling exactly where we are *today*—where we're failing today, as well as where we're succeeding. *"I'm as sick as my secrets,"* the saying goes. So we reveal our secrets; we bring the inside out. Self-honesty, in humility, yet so powerful. *We lead with our weaknesses.*
5. By continually working the principles of the Twelve Steps and Twelve Traditions in our lives first, and in our fellowship.
6. By helping others through identification. When we want to communicate to another member, we speak in terms of "I," not "we" or "you." We don't tell them what's wrong with them or give advice; *we relate what happened to us*. When we thus identify with another, it may not only help that person, but often reveals something about ourselves we've missed before. We don't tell; we share.

> *"I can* tell *you what's wrong with you without identifying, but this keeps me from looking at myself and can be destructive to you. But when I bring it up by identifying through my own experience, it means I'm bringing myself out into the light."*

7. By taking responsibility for our own recovery. There's a difference between taking responsibility for our recovery and being in charge of it. When we take responsibility, we've stopped saying "Fix me" and are willing to take the actions necessary to get well. We're

willing to take direction and work the Steps. This same attitude is what leads us to tie in to another sober member as helper or sponsor—one who can help us learn how to work the Steps in our daily lives. When we remain "in charge," however, we're shutting ourselves off from the light and help of other recovering members.

8. By leading with our weakness. There is an attractive healing atmosphere in meetings when someone is transparent, naive, "innocent," and self-revealing at depth. He or she may even be a newcomer, which is often the case and why we need them to help keep us honest. Vulnerable, and like a child, we take the supreme risk of exposing the truth about ourselves, dark as it may be. We lead with our weakness because that's where we're hurting, and *this* becomes the point of our identification with each other, the point of true union. Once this single ray of light shines in a meeting, it finds ready reception and response in the others present. Honesty is catching; we're learning to walk in the light.
9. By commitment to the group. SA members commit themselves to SA meetings. We attend every meeting we can. On time. Meetings, on time. Why this emphasis?

    When the meeting is handled in a haphazard manner, there's a feeling of What's the use? There's the feeling of being let down, that the secretary, leader, or other members don't care and are not really a *part of*. And if there's no feeling of mutual caring, then *I* can't be a *part of*. How can I become a part of something that's always shifting around? A feeling of separation and isolation comes into play—deadly for us.

    Meetings starting on time and a general orderliness are one of the legacies we've gotten from the best of other Twelve Step programs. Instead of "doing our own thing," which characterizes our self-obsession, we commit ourselves to every meeting and to being on time. No matter what—spouses, jobs, money—we put the group first because we put our own sobriety first. *Commitment to sobriety is commitment to the fellowship of sobriety.*

Meeting Guidelines

We can benefit from the unwritten guidelines that have contributed so profoundly to the success of other Twelve Step program meetings and have proven as valuable in our own.

1. Leaders of meetings are *servants* of that meeting. They don't "carry" the meeting; they merely facilitate it. A common mistake of those who have no prior Twelve Step meeting experience is to feel they must comment on everything that is said or "help out" in some way by giving "the answer." The effective leader surrenders this impulse and lets the meeting work itself.
2. The leader of the meeting does not have to acknowledge a raised hand; he or she can call on someone else. They can interrupt the one talking, if it is called for. This is in line with our common tradition. At the same time, a good meeting is one where the leader's presence is inconspicuous and noncontrolling.
3. Most groups stick with a certain basic set of readings that are read at every meeting, adding to this to suit the particular meeting. A list of suggested readings from which to draw is included in the Suggested Meeting Format. We use authorized SA and AA literature only, both for use during meetings and for distribution on the literature table.
4. Participation guidelines:

    - There is no cross talk. We don't interrupt others. However, the leader has the right to remind the person sharing of guidelines, time consumed, etc.
    - We don't give advice. We talk in the "I," not the "we" or the "you," speaking from our own experience. If we want to respond to what someone has said, we do so only in terms of our own experience. "I can only speak for myself, but whenever I did such and such, this is what happened in my life . . ."
    - We don't get carried away analyzing what caused our behavior or attitudes. If we were victimized

in early life, we slowly learn to face and work through it in acknowledgment, acceptance, and forgiveness. We talk as those who are now responsible for our attitudes and actions and are willing to take responsibility for our lives and recovery.

- In sharing, rather than displaying our knowledge or insights, we lead with our weakness and give of ourselves.
- We avoid politics, religious dogma, and other divisive issues. We also avoid explicit sexual descriptions and sexually abusive language.
- We avoid dumping, self-pity, and blaming others.
- We don't take the "inventories" of others; that is, we uncover and work on our own defects, not those of others. We refer to our own experiences.
- We *do* speak honestly of where we really are *today*. We try to develop transparent honesty of complete self-disclosure, letting the other members know where we are currently, regardless of length of sobriety.
- We *do* lead with our weakness and take the risk of total self-disclosure.
- By attending on time and sharing regularly, we *give* of ourselves to others in the group. We get back recovery.

(See the material under the heading "I Am a Sexaholic" under Step One, in this book, and read the article "Meeting Quality and Use of Non-SA Literature," in *Discovering the Principles.*)

The Sobriety Definition

Tradition Three states that "The only requirement for membership is a desire to stop lusting and become sexually sober." Given this requirement, one might think that sexual sobriety would be a relative matter that we define for ourselves. On the surface, this might appear to be an attractive and democratic idea. We think not.

Our rationalizations are ingenious. We tried masturbation only, or having "meaningful relationships" only, or having affairs where we "truly cared" for the other person. Or, we resorted only to one-nighters, prostitutes, or anonymous sex "so nobody got hurt." Over the long haul, these forms of experimentation did not work for us. There was no real *recovery*. Sobriety works for us.

How can we consider ourselves sober if we are still resorting to whatever or whomever we are using addictively? With most of us coming in, there was never any doubt what we had to stop doing. We *knew*. However, if we come into an SA group where we can define our own sobriety, watch those rationalizations come alive! And if we define our own level of sobriety, that's all we're likely to reach.

In defining sobriety, we do not speak for those outside Sexaholics Anonymous. We can only speak for ourselves. Thus, for the married sexaholic, sexual sobriety means having no form of sex with self or with persons other than the spouse. For the unmarried sexaholic, sexual sobriety means freedom from sex of any kind. And for all of us, single and married alike, *sexual sobriety also includes progressive victory over lust.* *

Of course, we recognize that one can be sexually "dry" but not sober from lust or dependency. The "dry drunk" syndrome, discovered in AA, applies to us as well, single or married. But we try to avoid passing judgment on the quality of another's inner sobriety. That must come from the individual. And if such persons keep coming back, the fact of whether or not they are living free from the power of sexual lust, fantasy, or dependency, not to mention switching addictions, usually becomes apparent. This aspect of recovery seems to be progressive. Thus, our SA expression: "True sobriety includes progressive victory over lust." But progress we must or recovery eludes us! The real problem for all of us—single, married, man, woman, from whatever lifestyle—is one and the same: the spiritual misconnection.

We have found that more important than the mere length of our calendar sobriety is its quality and our own personal integrity. Physical sobriety is not an end in itself but a means toward an end—victory over the obsession and progress in recovery. We are often the only ones who know on the inside of our souls whether we are truly in sobriety and recovery. (It is also possible we can be fooling ourselves.) Better to acknowledge where we really are than hide behind the badge of our sobriety date, cheat ourselves, and threaten our union with one another.

The fact that marrieds can have sex with their spouse and call themselves "sober" is no advantage at all. It can even work *against* recovery. Some marrieds confess that even though they aren't "acting out" any more, victory over lust still eludes them. As a matter of fact, it often seems harder for marrieds to get victory over lust and dependency unless they go through the experience of total sexual abstinence. And more often than we might suppose, marrieds

---

*In SA's sobriety definition, the term "spouse" refers to one's partner in a marriage between a man and a woman.

can be heard complaining that singles have it easier! Let's face it: sexaholics—recovering or not, single or married—can expect to have problems with sex! Not to mention the host of other problems entailed in trying to live with and relate to others.

What we strive toward is not only the negative sobriety of not acting out our sexaholism, but progressive victory over the obsession in the looking and thinking. We also strive toward the positive sobriety of acting out true union of persons. The great blessing (or curse, as the case may be) of our condition is that unless and until we can give unconditionally and relate with others, the vacuum left inside us from withdrawal will never be filled. All along, we had thought we could make the Connection by taking; we see now that we get it by giving. Our whole concept of sex begins to change. Sex finds a simple and natural place it could never have before and becomes merely one of the things that flows *from* true union in committed marriage. And even here, we've discovered that sex is optional.

Unity in fellowship and good spiritual quality in meetings are supported by this definition. Without defining sexual sobriety, we would make it possible for those who are still practicing lust in some fashion to lead meetings and hold policy-making positions affecting not only the group but SA as a whole. This could also compromise the spiritual atmosphere so that the power of God's presence would not be active in the meetings and fellowship. While groups may stay together without a commitment to sobriety—just as individuals may temporarily feel better without it—we have found that there is no true spiritual unity in groups without a shared commitment to sobriety and progress in recovery. *"Personal recovery depends on SA unity"* (Tradition One). Sobriety and victory over lust are the bases for our unity and common welfare, which must come first. Our sobriety is the *sine qua non*, the necessary basis of our recovery and fellowship. Without experiencing it, we have nothing.

For us, sobriety works.

We "Live and Let Live," but we do not call one another sober unless we are practicing sobriety.

APPENDIXES

APPENDIX 1

SA Meeting Formats

SUGGESTED MEETING FORMAT

1. "Good evening; my name is ______________ , and I'm a recovering sexaholic. Welcome to this meeting of Sexaholics Anonymous."

2. "This is a closed meeting. Only those desiring their own personal sexual sobriety, please."

"This is also a no smoking meeting; we ask that any smoking be done outside the meeting area, please."

3. LEADER ASKS SOMEONE TO READ "The SA Purpose."

4. LEADER ASKS SOMEONE TO READ "What Is a Sexaholic and What Is Sexual Sobriety?"

5. "Let's take a minute to introduce ourselves by first name and state our length of sexual sobriety. I'll begin, and we'll go around the room.
My name is ____________________ , I'm a sexaholic, and I've been sexually sober for ____________________ .

6. "Will you please join me in the serenity prayer. 'God, grant me the serenity to accept the things I cannot change, courage to change the things I can, and wisdom to know the difference.' "

7. LEADER ASKS FOR PERSONS TO READ TWO OR THREE SELECTIONS:
(Select readings beforehand.) Pick two or three from the following list: "The Problem," "The Solution," portion of Chapter 5 (AA), The Twelve Steps, The Twelve Traditions, or portions from *Sexaholics Anonymous*, Meeting Guide, brochure, or other SA or AA literature.

* 8. LEADER READS:
"In participation, we avoid topics that can lead to dissension or distraction. We also avoid explicit sexual descriptions and sexually abusive language. The emphasis is on honesty, recovery, and healing—how to apply the Twelve Steps and Traditions in our daily lives."
"No cross talk, please. If someone feels another is getting too explicit, they may so signify by quietly raising their hand."

9. LEADER BEGINS PARTICIPATION OR CALLS ON SOMEONE ELSE.

10. (At conclusion of participation) "It's time for our Seventh Tradition. While we pass the basket, do we have any announcements from the secretary?" (PASS THE BASKET) "We have no dues or fees but we are self-supporting through our own contributions."

11. Have someone read The Twelve Traditions of SA, unless done above.

**The following optional procedure has been found helpful by some groups:*
"All participants in the first part of this meeting will be members of SA who have been sexually sober for 30 days or more. We do this to help set the tone on recovery and program. After that, any member may share."

12. CLOSING STATEMENT. "Anything you have heard at this meeting is strictly the opinion of the individual participant; the principles of SA are found in our Twelve Steps and Twelve Traditions.

"This is an anonymous program. Please keep the name, address, and phone number of anyone you meet or learn about in SA to yourself. And what we say here, let it stay here."

"Remember that we never identify ourselves publicly with SA in the press, radio, TV, or films. Neither does anyone speak *for* SA."

13. LEADER READS OR ASKS SOMEONE TO READ "A Vision for you" or "The Twelve Promises."

14. "After a moment of silent meditation, I'd like to ask ____________________ to lead us in the Lord's Prayer." (Stand and hold hands in a circle.) "KEEP COMING BACK!"

SUGGESTED FORMAT FOR BOOK- OR STEP-STUDY MEETINGS

(Substitute the following for item 7 in the participation meeting format.)

"We read from *Sexaholics Anonymous* or the *Twelve Steps and Twelve Traditions* or both. We go around the table, each person reading one or more paragraphs, until we've read through the portion we have set for ourselves (either the whole chapter or portion thereof). The leader then opens it up to discussion. The aim is to see how we can learn to apply the Step and use it in our own lives. We try always to see the difference between mere understanding and belief and actually putting that principle into action in all areas of our lives."

APPENDIX 2

Readings Commonly Used in Meetings

THE SA PURPOSE

Sexaholics Anonymous is a fellowship of men and women who share their experience, strength, and hope with each other that they may solve their common problem and help others to recover. The only requirement for membership is a desire to stop lusting and become sexually sober. There are no dues or fees for SA membership; we are self-supporting through our own contributions. SA is not allied with any sect, denomination, politics, organization, or institution; does not wish to engage in any controversy; neither endorses nor opposes any causes. Our primary purpose is to stay sexually sober and help others to achieve sexual sobriety.

(Reprinted for adaptation with permission of the Alcoholics Anonymous *Grapevine*. Copyright The AA Grapevine, Inc.)

WHAT IS A SEXAHOLIC AND WHAT IS SEXUAL SOBRIETY?

We can only speak for ourselves. The specialized nature of Sexaholics Anonymous can best be understood in terms of what we call the *sexaholic*. The sexaholic has taken himself or herself out of the whole context of what is right or wrong. He or she has lost control, no longer has the power of choice, and is not free to stop. Lust has become an addiction. Our situation is like that of the alcoholic who can no longer tolerate alcohol and must stop drinking altogether but is hooked and cannot stop. So it is with the sexaholic, or sex drunk, who can no longer tolerate lust but cannot stop.

Thus, *for the sexaholic*, any form of sex with one's self or with partners other than the spouse is progressively addictive and destructive. We also see that lust is the driving force behind our sexual acting out, and true sobriety includes progressive victory over lust. These conclusions were forced upon us in the crucible of our experiences and recovery; we have no other options. But we have found that acceptance of these facts is the key to a happy and joyous freedom we could otherwise never know.

This will and should discourage many inquirers who admit to sexual obsession or compulsion but who simply want to control and enjoy it, much as the alcoholic would like to control and enjoy drinking. Until we had been driven to the point of despair, until we really wanted to stop but could not, we did not give ourselves to this program of recovery. Sexaholics Anonymous is for those who know they have no other option but to stop, and their own enlightened self-interest must tell them this.

THE PROBLEM

Many of us felt inadequate, unworthy, alone, and afraid. Our insides never matched what we saw on the outsides of others.

Early on, we came to feel disconnected—from parents, from peers, from ourselves. We tuned out with fantasy and masturbation. We plugged in by drinking in the pictures, the images, and pursuing the objects of our fantasies. We lusted and wanted to be lusted after.

We became true addicts: sex with self, promiscuity, adultery, dependency relationships, and more fantasy. We got it through the eyes; we bought it, we sold it, we traded it, we gave it away. We were addicted to the intrigue, the tease, the forbidden. The only way we knew to be free of it was to do it. "Please connect with me and make me whole!" we cried with outstretched arms. Lusting after the Big Fix, we gave away our power to others.

This produced guilt, self-hatred, remorse, emptiness, and pain, and we were driven ever inward, away from reality, away from love, lost inside ourselves.

Our habit made true intimacy impossible. We could never know real union with another because we were addicted to the *un*real. We went for the "chemistry," the connection that had the magic, *because* it bypassed intimacy and true union. Fantasy corrupted the real; lust killed love.

First addicts, then love cripples, we took from others to fill up what was lacking in ourselves. Conning ourselves time and again that the next one would save us, we were really losing our lives.

THE SOLUTION

We saw that our problem was threefold: physical, emotional, and spiritual. Healing had to come about in all three.

The crucial change in attitude began when we admitted we were powerless, that our habit had us whipped. We came to meetings and withdrew from our habit. For some, this meant no sex with themselves or others, including not getting into relationships. For others it also meant "drying out" and not having sex with the spouse for a time to recover from lust.

We discovered that we *could* stop, that not feeding the hunger didn't kill us, that sex was indeed optional. There was hope for freedom, and we began to feel alive. Encouraged to continue, we turned more and more away from our isolating obsession with sex and self and turned to God and others.

All this was scary. We couldn't see the path ahead, except that others had gone that way before. Each new step of surrender felt it would be off the edge into oblivion, but we took it. And instead of killing us, surrender was killing the obsession! We had stepped into the light, into a whole new way of life.

The fellowship gave us monitoring and support to keep us from being overwhelmed, a safe haven where we could finally face ourselves. Instead of covering our feelings with compulsive sex, we began exposing the roots of our spiritual emptiness and hunger. And the healing began.

As we faced our defects, we became willing to change; surrendering them broke the power they had over us. We began to be more comfortable with ourselves and others for the first time without our "drug."

Forgiving all who had injured us, and without injuring others, we tried to right our own wrongs. At each amends more of the dreadful load of guilt dropped from our shoulders, until we could lift our heads, look the world in the eye, and stand free.

We began practicing a positive sobriety, taking the actions of love to improve our relations with others. We were learning how to give; and the measure we gave was the measure we got back. We were finding what none of the substitutes had ever supplied. We were making the real Connection. We were home.

FROM CHAPTER FIVE OF *ALCOHOLICS ANONYMOUS*

Rarely have we seen a person fail who has thoroughly followed our path. Those who do not recover are people who cannot or will not completely give themselves to this simple program, usually men and women who are constitutionally incapable of being honest with themselves. There are such unfortunates. They are not at fault; they seem to have been born that way. They are naturally incapable of grasping and developing a manner of living which demands rigorous honesty. Their chances are less than average. There are those, too, who suffer from grave emotional and mental disorders, but many of them do recover if they have the capacity to be honest.

Our stories disclose in a general way what we used to be like, what happened, and what we are like now. If you have decided you want what we have and are willing to go to any length to get it, then you are ready to take certain steps.

At some of these we balked. We thought we could find an easier, softer way. But we could not. With all the earnestness at our command, we beg of you to be fearless and thorough from the very start. Some of us have tried to hold on to our old ideas, and the result was nil until we let go absolutely.

Remember that we deal with lust—cunning, baffling, and powerful! Without help it is too much for us. But there is One who has all power—that one is God. May you find Him now.

Half measures availed us nothing. We stood at the turning point. We asked His protection and care with complete abandon. Here are the steps we took, which are suggested as a program of recovery:

1. We admitted that we were powerless over lust—that our lives had become unmanageable.

2. Came to believe that a Power greater than ourselves could restore us to sanity.
3. Made a decision to turn our will and our lives over to the care of God *as we understood Him.*
4. Made a searching and fearless moral inventory of ourselves.
5. Admitted to God, to ourselves, and to another human being the exact nature of our wrongs.
6. Were entirely ready to have God remove all these defects of character.
7. Humbly asked Him to remove our shortcomings.
8. Made a list of all persons we had harmed, and became willing to make amends to them all.
9. Made direct amends to such people wherever possible, except when to do so would injure them or others.
10. Continued to take personal inventory and when we were wrong promptly admitted it.
11. Sought through prayer and meditation to improve our conscious contact with God *as we understood Him,* praying only for knowledge of His will for us and the power to carry that out.
12. Having had a spiritual awakening as the result of these Steps, we tried to carry this message to sexaholics and to practice these principles in all our affairs.

Many of us exclaimed, "What an order! I can't go through with it." Do not be discouraged. No one among us has been able to maintain anything like perfect adherence to these principles. We are not saints. The point is, that we are willing to grow along spiritual lines. The principles we have set down are guides to progress. We claim spiritual progress rather than spiritual perfection. . . . Our personal adventures before and after make clear three pertinent ideas:

(a) That we were sexaholics and could not manage our own lives.
(b) That probably no human power could have relieved our sexaholism.
(c) That God could and would if He were sought.

THE TWELVE STEPS OF SEXAHOLICS ANONYMOUS

1. We admitted that we were powerless over lust—that our lives had become unmanageable.
2. Came to believe that a Power greater than ourselves could restore us to sanity.
3. Made a decision to turn our will and our lives over to the care of God *as we understood Him.*
4. Made a searching and fearless moral inventory of ourselves.
5. Admitted to God, to ourselves, and to another human being the exact nature of our wrongs.
6. Were entirely ready to have God remove all these defects of character.
7. Humbly asked Him to remove our shortcomings.
8. Made a list of all persons we had harmed, and became willing to make amends to them all.
9. Made direct amends to such people wherever possible, except when to do so would injure them or others.
10. Continued to take personal inventory and when we were wrong promptly admitted it.
11. Sought through prayer and meditation to improve our conscious contact with God *as we understood Him*, praying only for knowledge of His will for us and the power to carry that out.
12. Having had a spiritual awakening as the result of these Steps, we tried to carry this message to sexaholics, and to practice these principles in all our affairs.

THE TWELVE TRADITIONS OF SEXAHOLICS ANONYMOUS

1. Our common welfare should come first; personal recovery depends on SA unity.
2. For our group purpose there is but one ultimate authority—a loving God as He may express Himself in our group conscience. Our leaders are but trusted servants; they do not govern.
3. The only requirement for membership is a desire to stop lusting and become sexually sober.
4. Each group should be autonomous except in matters affecting other groups or Sexaholics Anonymous as a whole.
5. Each group has but one primary purpose—to carry its message to the sexaholic who still suffers.
6. An SA group ought never endorse, finance, or lend the SA name to any related facility or outside enterprise, lest problems of money, property, and prestige divert us from our primary purpose.
7. Every SA group ought to be fully self-supporting, declining outside contributions.
8. Sexaholics Anonymous should remain forever non-professional, but our service centers may employ special workers.
9. SA, as such, ought never be organized; but we may create service boards or committees directly responsible to those they serve.
10. Sexaholics Anonymous has no opinion on outside issues; hence the SA name ought never be drawn into public controversy.
11. Our public relations policy is based on attraction rather than promotion; we need always maintain personal anonymity at the level of press, radio, films, and TV.
12. Anonymity is the spiritual foundation of all our traditions, ever reminding us to place principles before personalities.

A VISION FOR YOU

We realize we know only a little. God will constantly disclose more to you and to us. Ask Him in your morning meditation what you can do each day for the man who is still sick. The answers will come, if your own house is in order. But obviously you cannot transmit something you haven't got. See to it that your relationship with Him is right, and great events will come to pass for you and countless others. This is the Great Fact for us.

Abandon yourself to God as you understand God. Admit your faults to Him and to your fellows. Clear away the wreckage of your past. Give freely of what you find and join us. We shall be with you in the Fellowship of the Spirit, and you will surely meet some of us as you trudge the Road of Happy Destiny.

May God bless you and keep you—until then.

(*Alcoholics Anonymous*, p.164)

THE SERENITY PRAYER

God grant me the serenity to accept the things I cannot change, courage to change the things I can, and wisdom to know the difference.

APPENDIX 3

Where to Go For More Information

Making Contact with Groups in Your Area

1. Try your local area telephone directory or information operator or ask for directory information in a large neighboring city. Increasing numbers of SA groups are placing listings in local or area telephone directories.

2. Contact the Sexaholics Anonymous Central Office, which handles our world services. This is our most complete service with the most up-to-date listing of groups and contacts.

3. All new and existing SA groups are urged to list themselves with the SA Central Office so inquirers in their areas may be referred to contacts. Contact the Central Office, listed below, and provide names and phone numbers of one or more contacts for your group. This also makes it possible for the Central Office to send news of matters affecting SA as a whole, which should be made available to all members.

Literature

This book, *Sexaholics Anonymous*, and other items such as the SA brochure, *Recovery Continues*, *Discovering the Principles,* other literature, tapes, CDs, and the *Essay* newsletter are available at local SA groups or can be ordered directly from the SA Central Office or website, listed below. Contact the Central Office or go to the website for current literature and prices. AA literature can be obtained from any local AA office or group or from the AA General Service Office, Box 459 Grand Central Station, NY, NY, 10163.

SA Newsletter

The Sexaholics Anonymous newsletter, *Essay*, is issued periodically. Members are urged to contact the Central Office and ask to be placed on the mailing list. The Essay has a Calendar of Events section, describing the various conventions, marathons, retreats, and other regional, national, or international SA functions that take place throughout the year. Sections on Group and Member News provide excerpts from letters around the world on group and member experiences. The *Essay* also contains Central Office news and financial reports and news of matters affecting the whole fellowship, with articles on various subjects and personal experiences reflecting what is happening in SA. *Essay* has proven to be an important channel of recovery and link for union of our fellowship at the broader levels—something that has become rewarding to a great many of us.

For more information about SA write:

SA, P.O.B. 3565, Brentwood, TN 37024-3565
Phone: 615-370-6062, FAX: 615-370-0882
e-mail: saico@sa.org
All SA literature may be ordered from the SA website at
www.sa.org